THE INCREDIBLE ESSENCE OF ELEPHANTS

CHANGARAM S. VENUGOPAL

AND

JACOB V. CHEERANL

ISBN: 979-8-89216-008-7 (Paperback)
979-8-89216-009-4 (E-book)

Library of Congress Control Number: 2024906393

BookmarcAlliance
California, USA
www.bookmarcalliance.com

DEDICATION

This book is dedicated to all elephants, African and Asian. Dear "elefriends," we love each and every one of you for your human-like characteristics, such as intelligence, memory, talent, love, and compassion.

PREFACE

Almost sixty years ago the authors met at the Kerala Veterinary College and Research Institute, Kerala State, India. Dr. Jacob V. Cheeran was in his second year and Dr. Changaram Venugopal was in his first year. In the late '60's, they were reunited again at the same college, where they were both doing post graduate studies in pharmacology under the same major advisor, Dr. K.P.D. Nair. Dr. Nair was the head of the department. Dr. Cheeran was a faculty member and was completing his post graduate studies on a part-time basis. Dr. Venugopal, a full-time graduate student, was investigating the effect of skeletal muscle relaxants in immobilizing domestic animals. After graduating in 1971, Dr. Venugopal went on to study at the Indian Veterinary Research Institute, New Delhi and then to the United States for advanced studies in pharmacology.

Meanwhile in India in the 1970s, there were many incidents of elephants running amok from festivals in temples. The elephants were causing a lot of property damage as well as endangering the human population. This resulted in a state-wide commotion and public uproar against the use of elephants in festivals. The Veterinary College was approached to come up with a solution to the elephant problem. Dr. Nair, realizing the severity of the issue, took it upon himself to the purchase a "capture gun," which had to be imported from another country. Since this was a major decision, which involved a Customs Department import license, Dr. Nair had to get permissions from the central government. After a couple of years, with the support of his fellow faculty members, including Dr. Cheeran, he was able to successfully justify the purchase of the capture gun to the government. In a short time, the procurement of the capture gun became a reality.

Dr. Nair had to retire before he could complete his mission. He passed on his responsibilities to Dr. Cheeran. Dr. Cheeran was able to use the capture gun to tranquilize elephants and later also became the head of the Pharmacology Department. It took many training sessions to become a proficient sharp shooter using the capture gun and he was able to successfully use this skill to tranquilize Elephants in musth. Dr. Cheeran, with the help of two other faculty members (Dr. Kaimal and Dr. Panicker), formed a team for capturing elephants that run amok during musth. They continued in this field of veterinary service for seven years. Dr. Cheeran also collaborated with Dr. P.O. George, professor of surgery in the college and a zoo veterinarian at Thrissur, Kerala State.

Later, the Kerala Agricultural University appointed Dr. Cheeran as the Chairman of the Elephant Study Center, because of his elephant expertise. He was also an appointed member of the Steering Committee of Project Elephant and of the Central Zoo authority by the Government of India. Then he had to extend his services nationally and internationally. His duties involved travelling to other states in India; training veterinary and wildlife officers; leading a team for elephant relocating projects; and implementing radio collars for wild elephants and other wild animals, including wild buffaloes, in the entire country. He had to travel to the US, Thailand, and Australia for seminars, conferences, and court hearings on elephants. His encounters with elephants were adventurous and some were even life-threatening. This gave him ample experience, confidence, and expertise in chemical immobilization of elephants and helped him to determine the immobilizing dose of tranquilizers for various wild animals, including elephants.

Dr. Venugopal kept in touch with Dr. Cheeran and discussed the latest information about elephants. They exchanged the information internationally. Dr. Cheeran gave a lecture at the Smithsonian Institute, Washington, DC, and then made a special trip to Louisiana State University School of Veterinary Medicine in Baton Rouge, LA, where Dr. Venugopal taught, to give a lecturer-seminar on elephant immobilization to the students and faculty. They continued to collaborate even after Dr. Venugopal retired from LSU after thirty-three years of teaching and research.

All these experiences gave Dr. Cheeran opportunities to have close contacts with captive as well as wild elephants. During his tenure as the Chairman of Elephant Study Center, he tranquilized more than five hundred elephants in musth and several wild elephants for relocation. He treated many elephants that came to the teaching hospitals of the College with various ailments.

Dr. Cheeran started writing articles about elephants for the local newspapers and weekly magazines in his native language, Malayalam. Later, due to the heart-felt requests from the public, he compiled them and published this information as a book in Malayalam. Recently, the enthusiastic readers requested him to translate the book into English so that people in other states in India, as well as those around the world would benefit with this information. Dr. Venugopal read the book and they decided to collaborate on the book translation with the permission of H & C Publishers. They also added various new topics on elephants into the book in English.

Since both authors are veterinarians specialized in pharmacology, they are familiar with the tranquilizers, their mechanism of action, and tranquilization of elephants. This book combines the scientific information with interesting facts about elephants. Both authors are ardent lovers of elephants and want to share their passion and knowledge with other people. Although elephants are considered sacred, compassionate animals, they are mistreated by opportunistic people. The authors would like to see elephants treated with fairness, love, sympathy, and consideration they deserve. The authors want to thank all those helped them to make their dream come true.

Dr. Changaram S. Venugopal
Dr. Jacob V. Cheeran

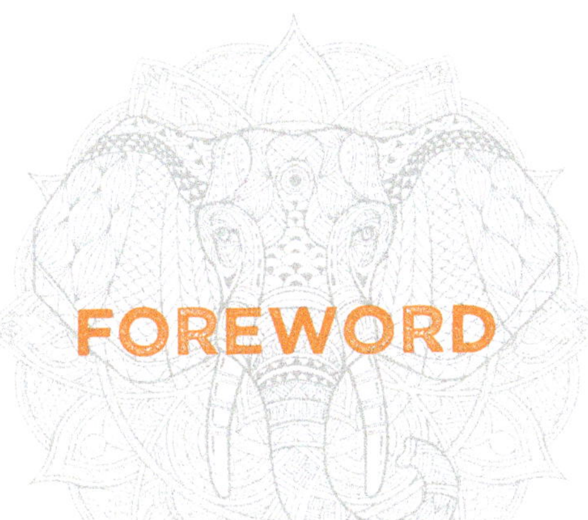

FOREWORD

I AM HONORED TO have been asked to write the foreword for *The Incredible Essence of Elephants*, written by my long-time colleagues, Dr. Cheeran and Dr. Venugopal. I share their passion for elephants and their dedication to advancing our knowledge of this most significant species.

The *Incredible Essence of Elephants* is both educational and entertaining, and will be enjoyed by elephant lovers of all ages, as well as scientists, veterinarians, and students. It provides a broad perspective of the life and lore of both Asian and African elephants.

The nine chapters that comprise the book cover diverse topics, including the origins of elephants, their biology, famous elephants, human interventions in elephants' lives, and much more. Each chapter offers the reader insights into the unique lives of the two veterinarian-authors as they intertwine scientific facts with their personal experiences.

Chapter 2 offers the reader eleven fascinating stories from the annals of elephants in history. We learn about Alexander the Great's encounter with elephants in war and Thomas Jefferson's fascination with elephants that led him to send the famous explorers Lewis and Clarke to Kentucky to excavate elephant bones (later identified as mastodons).

I especially enjoyed Chapter 3, "Life of Elephants." The section "Human-Like Characteristics in Elephants" captured the essence of the similarities between our two species. This chapter is rich with anecdotes from the authors' first-hand experiences. The description of a funeral and elephants mourning after the death of a herd-mate in Botswana was especially poignant. At the end of the narration, the authors pose these questions: Was this a memorial service or a routine funeral service for the dead among elephants? Do elephants have emotions and sorrows? Do they express their compassion and sorrows like human beings or even more so? Certainly these questions cause the reader to also ponder the answers.

Chapter 3 also has stories about love and compassion and the importance of elephant grandmothers—another similarity to our own species. And don't miss reading about the challenges and surprises that can happen when tranquilizing wild elephants. Dr. Cheeran is an expert in tranquilization and has probably tranquilized more Asian elephants than anyone in the world!

For the science-minded, Chapter 4 is all about elephant biology.

In Chapter 5, the authors present some of the many talents of elephants that make them so unique. Did you know that elephants can hear with their feet? That they dig wells? Everyone knows elephants are smart and the mirror test proves it. Elephants can recognize themselves in a mirror. This ranks elephants together with other smart species like chimpanzees and dolphins that also pass this intelligence test. These are just some of the interesting facts you will find in this chapter.

"Problems in elephants" is the subject of the next chapter. Many animals are known to like alcohol, and elephants are no exception. The authors describe the antics of inebriated elephants and drunkard elephants raiding a village. There is a sad story of elephants that became addicted to drugs at the hand of humans, but the story has a happy ending— the elephants were rescued, rehabilitated, and released. Fascinating facts about musth are conveyed and we hear how one old lady "conquered" an elephant in musth with love (and food).

Important elephants are featured in Chapter 7, including the world-famous "Jumbo." We are introduced to a very old elephant who was honored with the title "Grandmother of Elephants" and we learn about the lives of temple elephants. The authors talk about elephants that were given LSD—a pointless experiment and a tragic example of bad science. On a more positive note, we learn the truth about white elephants and their true origin—you will have to read the chapter to find out!

The elephant population crisis in Africa, human-elephant conflict in West Bengal, and how special rats have made trails safe for elephants in parts of Africa are discussed in Chapter 8.

Wild and captive elephants are the subject of the final chapter. We learn more about how elephants were used in war and about temple elephants in Kerala. Mating rituals is another subject and we learn that a wild elephant who has had his tail bitten off may have lost a fight for mating privileges. The book concludes with Words of Wisdom from the two authors and some additional factoids, like what it means when a person is called a "downward directed tusker"—you will have to read the book to find out and I promise that you will enjoy every second!

Susan K. Mikota DVM
Dimplomate, American College of Animal Welfare
Elephant Care International
Director of Veterinary Programs and Research
www.elephantcare.org

July 2018

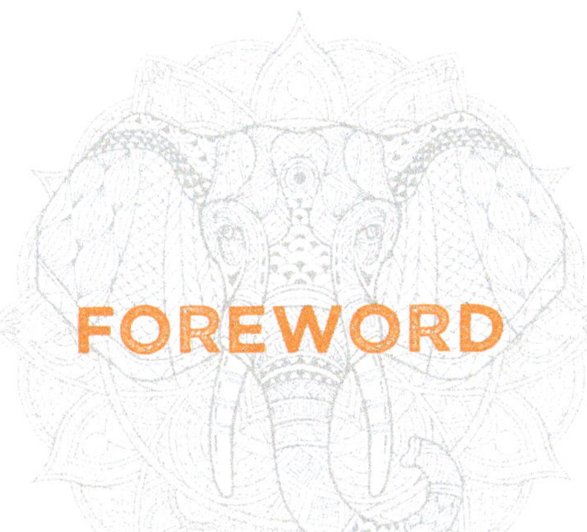

FOREWORD

ALTHOUGH A VETERINARIAN, I have no experience or expertise with elephants. When asked if I would provide a foreword for the *Incredible Essence of Elephants*, I was thus a bit hesitant. That was until Dr. Venugopal explained they wanted the perspective of someone without such expertise (a kind of non-expert review, because the book is targeted mainly toward elephant enthusiasts, students, elephant farm employees, and some veterinarians in elephant practice). It soon became an easy decision to get a pre-read of this fascinating book before its publication and to write a foreword. While reading the book I began reflecting and remembering my personal connection to elephants.

I have known Dr. Changaram Venugopal for twenty-four years. He is an amazing person and professional, a veterinarian, research scientist, mentor, role model, and was much more to so many people throughout his career. Originally from India, he came to the United States many years ago for graduate studies and then began as a faculty member at the Louisiana State University School of Veterinary Medicine in the 1980s. He worked there until his retirement in 2014. Although I don't know Dr. Jacob Cheeran personally, the fact that he has been a friend and colleague of Dr. Venugopal for many years and that they have collaborated on this book makes it all the more authentic and special. Likewise, it is clear from reading the book that he has vast clinical and research experience with and expertise about the elephants.

There have been books published on the topic of elephants or involving elephant characters, and to me none more enjoyable and informative than this book since *Water of Elephants*, which featured Rosie, the lovable, intelligent, loyal and good-natured elephant who only understood Polish and loved lemonade and gin and popcorn. Written by two veterinarians native to India, this book captures the energy, excitement, and essence of elephants.

This book is a masterful blend of research, science, unique facts, interesting trivia, and personal experiences and stories about elephants. It "pulls back the curtain" and sheds light on the majestic and mythical allure of elephants, from their origin, evolution, and history; anatomy, biology, and physiology; behavior, social habits, and family structure; intelligence, senses, and emotions; and much more. Similar to horses, they have no gall bladder. They have big ears, but they don't rely solely on them for their astute hearing. They detect vibrations and noises through sensors in their foot pads. They can detect water underground and dig wells when water sources have dried up. Unlike other non-primate mammals, their mammary glands are between their front legs. The oldest female in the herd is the leader, and like in people, grandmothers serve an important role in the family structure, often teaching how to raise the baby elephants, and even "baby sitting" and helping to raise them.

Elephants have been described to be some of the most social, creative, and benevolent animals on earth. With lifespans, emotions, intellect, memory, problem-solving abilities, and behaviors similar to humans, it is perhaps easy to understand why they are so endeared by people around the world. Unlike most animals, elephants have been shown to recognize their reflection in a mirror. They appear to mourn, grieve, and hold "funerals" or similar rituals for fellow elephants in their herd, including covering their remains. They are social and have symbiotic relationships with birds who ride around on their backs and get their meals from insects.

Similar to people, elephants can develop addictive behaviors either to things found in nature or those made by people, including heroin, other narcotics, alcohol, and more. They are one of the few species known to experience posttraumatic stress syndrome.

Information is woven throughout the book regarding several famous elephants. None more so than Jumbo, an elephant acquired by the London Zoo and then Purchased by P.T. Barnum and transported from London to the United States, where he went on exhibition and went on to became the start of "The Greatest Show on Earth" before his tragic death in 1885. Although unaware of this history about Jumbo until reading this book, it is noteworthy the first thought that came to my mind when asked to read and reflect on the book and prepare a foreword was about my experience with the Ringling Brothers and Barnum Bailey Circus when I was a young boy.

I vividly remember an encounter with circus elephants who were part of the Ringling Brothers and Barnum Bailey Circus, which was visiting Charleston, WV, in the early 1970s when I was approximately eight years old. My mother and great aunt took me and my two brothers. We had front row seats and when the elephants were in a line in front of us they turned to face the crowd and reared up on their hind legs. We all got sprayed with "elephant pee." I don't think we ever got seats in the front row again. A few rows back was safer.

Although in some African countries elephant populations have increased, it is sad that worldwide elephant populations have declined by over 60 percent in the last decade, and this book helps address some of factors that have led to this, including poaching and habitat encroachment.

Elephants have highly developed brains and have the largest of all land mammals, which helps facilitate their amazing memory. As the saying goes, elephants never forget nor do they forgive! Elephant brains are remarkably similar to human brains despite differences in the size of their brain in proportion to body mass.

Whether African or Asian, wild or captive, famous or unknown—what do all elephants have in common? These magnificent creatures have a majestic, magical, mysterious, and mythical allure! Whether you're an elephant aficionado or have no knowledge about elephants, you will find *The Incredible Essence of Elephants* engaging, enjoyable, enlightening, and educational. A must read!

Rustin M. Moore, DVM, PhD, Diplomate ACVS
Dean,College of Veterinary Medicine,The Ohio State University

ACKNOWLEDGEMENT

WE, THE AUTHORS, WOULD like to thank the following individuals for their help in making our dream a reality.

Ms. Kathleen Eckman, a retired nurse, an avid reader of fiction and non-fiction novels and a lifelong lover of animals, is the one who read the first draft of the manuscript. She spent a lot of time and did a wonderful job of editing several areas of the manuscript and changing the expressions and style of the manuscript. Our heart-felt thanks to her and her family.

We thank you Dr. Susan Mikota, who specialized in wildlife medicine, particularly related to elephant care and management. We thank her and appreciate her willingness to write a foreword for the book.

We thank Dr. Rustin Moore, the Dean of College of Veterinary Medicine at the Ohio State University for providing an excellent foreword explaining how he enjoyed reading the book without any experience with elephants.

We want to thank from the bottom of our heart our friends Ronda and Paul Duplessis, who spent their valuable time to read and evaluate the manuscript. Their suggestions were valuable in improving the quality of the book.

My heart-felt thanks are due to Dr. Camille Russo III, a retired dental surgeon, who evaluated the contents of the manuscript and made some valuable comments which helped us improve the readability of the book.

Ms. Jennifer Hill, Director of Social Programs of Catholic Charities of Baton Rouge, was instrumental in arriving at a title for the book. Her acumen for the use of appropriate terms to describe apt meaning of words is commendable. We thank her dearly.

We would like to thank the owner of H & C publishers, Mr. T.I. Varghese for giving permission to translate the information published in native tongue Malayalam.

Our heart-felt thanks are also due to our photographer Mr. Marshal Radhakrishnan for providing elephant photos for the book and Mr. Mahendra Kunju for devoting his valuable time in editing some of those photos.

Although the information furnished in the book is essentially from the authors' experiences, particularly those of Dr. Cheeran, as an elephant veterinarian, his discussion with experienced mahouts and elephant owners, we also gathered information from news media in print as well as in digital forms. We want to thank all sources that helped us in this endeavor.

Last,but not the least,we want to thank our family members listed below for their encouragement and their patience and tolerance to our aloofness from the family duties during the preparation of the book. The list includes Mrs. Shirley Jacob Cheeran, Mrs. Sheela Venugopal, Jay Venugopal and Ms. Rashmi Venugopal, particularly for Rashmi's help in various stages writing.

With sincere thanks,
Changaram S. Venugopal
Jacob V. Cheeran

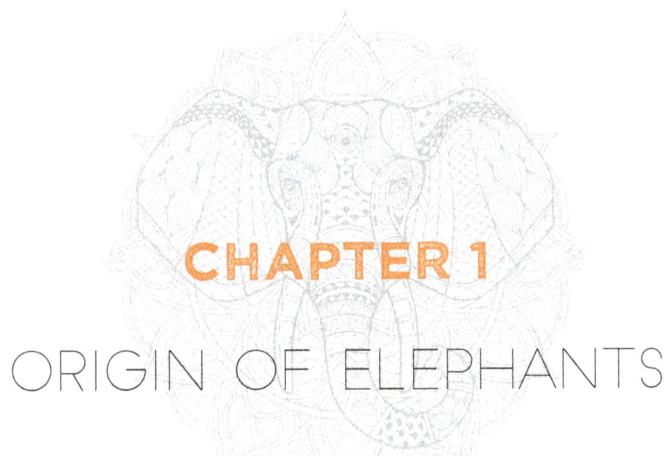

CHAPTER 1

ORIGIN OF ELEPHANTS

Evolution of elephants

It could be a coincidence that the evolution of elephants is associated with Egypt. This country is well-known for human civilization and considered to be the cradle of civilization of human kind, dating back several thousand years.

The ancestors of elephants are believed to be an animal about the size of a small hippopotamus, commonly seen in the marshy lands of Egypt. This creature had a long nose similar to a tapir, an herbivorous mammal more resembling a pig than today's elephant. Subsequent evolutionary changes brought this long nose to the present-day trunk. Scientists identified this animal by the name "moerithetherium" because the skeleton of these animals were first recovered from Lake Moeris, a lake that still exists about a hundred kilometers from Cairo. These animals became extinct approximately thirty million years ago; however, scientists believe that one hundred and fifty to three hundred species of animals living on earth were descendants of "moerithetherium."

The elephant we see today originated from mammoths which lived close to the end of the Ice Age. Mammoths had an unusually big body size, extremely long tusks, and long hair covering bodies. Almost ten thousand years ago, these animals migrated from the North Pole region to the southern tundra region. Their carcasses were discovered intact, without any deterioration, buried deep in the snow. These carcasses underwent extensive scientific research, which provided us information about the origin of elephants. We know that elephants migrated to almost all parts of the world except the continents of Australia and Antarctica; even today it is believed that thousands of tusks are buried deep in frozen ice in the snows of Siberia.

Currently, a land animal (hyraxes) and a sea animal (sea cows) are considered related to elephants based on biological similarities by evolutionary biologists. Asian elephants that once roamed the entire Asian continent are now seen only in India, Nepal, Bhutan, Bangladesh, Sri Lanka, Myanmar (Burma), Thailand, South China, Laos, Cambodia, Vietnam, Malaysia, and Indonesia. In India, they are seen only in the southern and eastern regions and the valleys of the Himalayas.

African elephants are found in countries of the African continent, particularly in mid-Africa (Zaire) and the eastern regions (Tanzania, Kenya, Ethiopia, Uganda, Sudan, Somalia, South Africa, Zimbabwe, Zambia, Namibia, and Malawi). It is estimated that the total number of African elephants are between three hundred Thousand to six hundred thousand, whereas Indian elephants number only between thirty-five thousand and forty-five thousand. In Africa, elephants in captivity are very few, whereas Indian elephants in captivity constitute about fifteen thousand (almost 50 percent). Recent censuses show that wild elephants in India may number from twenty-one thousand to twenty-five thousand. Next to India, most Asian elephants are seen in countries such as Myanmar, Thailand, Sri Lanka, and Sumatra. Although Laos (Lan Xang Kingdom) means “land of million elephants,”only little over one thousand elephants remain there. The population is decreasing globally at a rate that considers elephants an endangered species, and indicates that a time may come in the near future when we will only see elephants in zoos, paintings, or in the movies.

Types of elephants

Elephants belong to the family of Elephantidae in the animal kingdom. Broadly, two types of elephants exist in the world. They are the African elephants and the Asian or Indian elephants. The African elephants are of two sub types—those found in the savanna grass meadows and those found in the forest. The elephants in the forest are comparatively smaller than those found in the savanna grass meadows. Overall, all elephants can be classified as African bush elephants, African forest elephants, or Asian/Indian elephants. There are a lot of differences between African and Asian elephants. The most important difference is expressed in the size of their earlobes. The earlobes are larger in African elephants than Indian elephants.

The body size is also very large in African elephants. In the African elephants, both male and females have tusks, whereas in Asian elephants only males have tusks. With regards to the body hair, Asian elephants have more hair. The Savanna elephants are in general the largest in the world. The smallest elephants are the Asian elephants found in Sumatra, Indonesia (Bornean elephants).

The following table shows the list of major difference between African and Asian elephants

Characteristics	Asian Elephant	African Elephant
Weight	3-5 tons (3000-5000 pounds)	4-7 tons (4000-7000 pounds)
Height at shoulder	2-3.5 meters	3-4 meters
Tallest portion of body of the shoulder	On the top of head	In front (top)
Body shape	Straight back or slightly arching	Back curving inward
Abdomen	Hanging vertically/ sideways	Hanging from backwards

Head	Looks like an air sac pressed from sides with a central depression, three bumps on forehead	No pressed look and no central depression sloping forward
Ear	Smaller, does not go beyond shoulders, upper edge curves down to the front as elephant ages	Larger, taller than neck, curves backwards as elephant ages
Skin	Comparatively smoother, less wrinkled	More larger wrinkles
Ribs	19-20 pairs 33 caudal	20-21 pairs, 26 caudal
Teeth	Chewing surface with less wide oval circles	Chewing surface kidney-shaped
Tusk	Seen only in males; females and makhnas (males that have rudimentary tusks called tushes)	Present in males and females, smaller in females though
Trunk	Less rings, stronger, only one finger at the tip	More rings, more flexible two fingers at the tip

The following table shows differences between African Bush Elephants and African Forest Elephants

Characteristics	African Bush Elephant (Savanna)t	African Forest Elephant
Weight	4-7 tons (4000-7000 pounds)	2-4 tons (2000-4000 pounds)
Height at shoulder	3-4 meters	2-3 meters
Skin	Darker, more hair, particularly on trunks and around the mount	Less dark, less hair except in baby elephants
Ear shape	Triangular or trapezoidal	Circular
Tusk	More heavy, curvy	Less heavy, slender
Nails	Front leg: 4-5 Rear leg: 3-5	Front leg: 5 Rear leg: 4

Recently, scientists have suggested, but not confirmed, that there could be new subtype of elephants which evolved from the natural cross between Savana elephants and the forest elephants of Africa.

Is the elephant a "naked" animal?

Biologically speaking, an elephant is a "naked" animal. The hallmark of mammals is how their bodies are covered with hair. Monkeys, as the ancestors of humanity, have hair all over their bodies. However, when humans evolved we lost tails as well as our hair coverings. So much debate exists regarding the "nakedness" in humans also. Mr. Desmond Morris wrote a book about humans called *The Naked Ape*.

How did this happen to elephants? There are several views about it. Wooly mammoth, the ancestors of elephants, had hair all over their bodies. The word "mammoth" came from the Russian language. Mammoths had an average height of nine feet. It is interesting to note that their hair length was about 3.25 feet (more than a meter). They had a thick layer of subcutaneous fat, which protected them from the severe cold winters. They were inhabitants of extremely cold arctic region and became extinct about twelve thousand years ago. They lived in the era of Pleistocene or the Ice Age. Humans also originated during this time. Today, the skeleton and tusks of mammoths are found in the northern regions of Russia. It is estimated that several tons of skeletons and tusks of mammoths are buried deep in snow (frozen in the ice) in this area. Just like elephant tusks, mammoth tusks are used for making carved handicraft items.

Elephant, a corner stone of the ecosystem

Environmentalists and ecologists consider the elephant a corner stone of the environment because they are associated with plants and animals equally. They are an integral part to maintaining the ecological balance.

The role of elephants in maintaining the environment can be illustrated by several simple examples. In the wild, many birds live on the top of elephants. When elephants shake bushy plants and small branches of big trees to eat leaves, the insects and other small living creatures that inhabit these plants come out and fall onto the ground. The birds sitting on the back of the elephants take this opportunity to find their food. It is symbiotic life.

Another example is when elephants eat fruit and grains. Many times, the seeds of the fruits are not fully digested and they are excreted along with their dung. The grains and seeds in the dung are capable of germinating to new plants; the dung is a natural fertilizer. Seeds grow very well in that environment. Thus, elephants are known to be responsible for propagation of seed of more than thirty varieties of plants. The baboons in Africa search for the seeds in the dung for their food. Seeds of some Acacia plants can germinate only if their fruits are eaten and seeds are excreted by elephants. Since elephants walk for long distance, it is possible to see the germinated plants in the dung on the paths they travelled. However, it is interesting to note that these seeds will be digested and assimilated when eaten by monkeys. By the way, the coffee brewed from the beans excreted by elephants is more expensive.

The elephant dung eventually disintegrates and decays, and subsequently becomes a part of the soil. A huge number of microorganisms take the lead during the decaying process. Eight-legged insects such as beetles take an active role in converting the residues of dung to be blended with the soil. Some varieties of beetles are specific for elephant dung. Usually, the weight of these insects exceeds the weight of the dung itself. Another service rendered by elephants is that when they walk in the thick forests, they make small pathways which are used by other small animals.

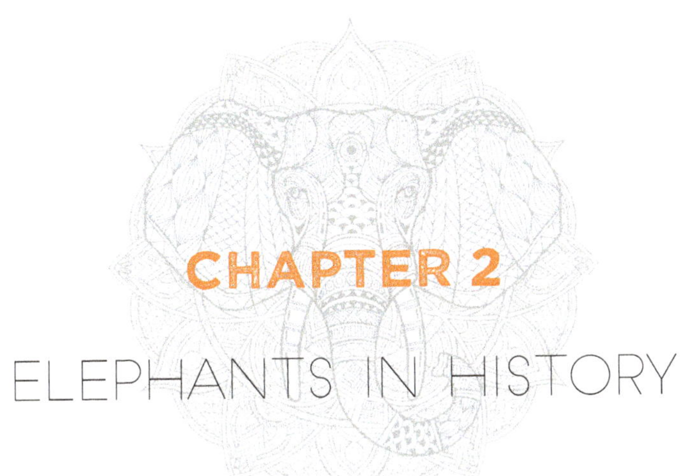

CHAPTER 2
ELEPHANTS IN HISTORY

Pachyderms of Pyrrhus

Alexander the Great was the first emperor of the Western world who encountered elephants in war. It was the time when he came to India and met King Porus, the king of eastern Punjab. Since then it became a custom for nobility and generals to keep elephants, but not necessarily for war. Actually, Westerners hardly had any idea how to train elephants for war and its accoutrements. King Pyrrhus (360-272 BC), the king of Epirus (modern Albania) wanted to revive Alexander's empire. Kindly Pyrrhus invaded southern Italy with twenty elephants. He hoped that the presence of elephants in his army would terrify the soldiers defending Rome. But these huge animals were actually blocking his army's advances, especially in narrow paths. Some of the elephants got frightened and bolted and trampled their own foot soldiers. With all the hurdles, he finally won the war at a great cost. This is responsible for the idiom "Pyrrhic victory." Plutarch, the ancient historian, made a satirical remark about this incident: "If we are victorious in one more battle with the Romans, we shall utterly be ruined."

Surus of Hannibal

Hannibal (247-182 BC), the Carthaginian general and statesman, and the son of Hamilcar Barca, is acknowledged as one of the greatest military generals. In 218 BC, he invaded Italy from the north, crossing the Alps from Gaul. His army was composed of foot soldiers, cavalry, and a few forest elephants of Africa. Only six elephants survived this difficulty mountain trek and five of the six died the following winter. The surviving elephant had only one tusk, which resembled Ganesh, the elephant God in Indian mythology. His name was Surus and he was Hannibal's mount. Riding atop an elephant served as a high platform, allowing Hannibal to see far beyond the marshes of Arno. During the next fifteen years, Hannibal won several battles and occupied large areas of Italy. It is believed he replenished the elephant herd in his army with new elephants from Africa.

There are two types of elephants in Africa. One, the popular Savanna elephant (*Loxodonta africana*) commonly seen in zoos. It is quite large and has huge ears which resemble the continent itself. The other is the forest elephant (*Loxodonta africana-cyclotis*), much smaller than the Savanna or the Asian elephant (*Elephas maximus*). Historians disagree on the type of elephant used by Hannibal. Discovery of coins released by Hannibal to commemorate his victories suggest he used the forest type of elephants in war. However, some historians believe he also used Asian elephants. In the battle with Roman Consul Marcellus in 209 BC, Hannibal's war elephants bolted, frightened and confused by the injuries inflicted on them by Roman soldiers. This is turn caused panic and threw his entire army in disarray.

Kandula

Kandula was an elephant who helped unification of Ceylon (present day Sri Lanka). He was the trusted mount of King Dutugamunu, who ruled Sri Lanka in the second century BC. The elephant Kandula was captured from the forest around the time of Dutugamunu's birth. Both the king and the elephant were raised alongside each other and became best friends. An incident in an Buddhist Chronicle "Mahavamsa" says that molten pitch somehow fell onto Kandula's body. The king was so grief stricken he cried as a baby and rushed to

Armor for elephant used in war

Kandula, applying ointment to the wound. He said, "Dear Kandula, I will make you the Lord of all Ceylon." After this, Kandula became the king's personal mount and was ridden in all the king's battles. His loyalty to his king as well as his performance in battle was heroic. In the siege of Vijitanagra around the year 161 BC, Kandula broke down the well-fortified gate while still covering from his wounds. Kandula participated in the king's battle against his sworn enemy, king Elara of India, who occupied the northern region of Sri Lanka. Dutugamunu, riding his beloved mount Kandula, defeated

King Elara on his mount Maha Pambati (meaning big rock). In a one-to-one combat, the victorious King Dutugamunu became the ruler of Sri Lanka with the help of Kandula.

Raja

This is an elephant that got the admiration of the entire country of Sri Lanka. Raja (meaning king) was a captive Asian male elephant whose name reached the level of world fame. His story is well-known in Sri Lanka. In Candy, a beautiful city in Sri Lanka, the people there have an auspicious and famous festival honoring Lord Buddha, whose teachings are the gospels of the religion. Although Buddha never advocated or supported the information of a religion, he is considered the founder of Buddhism, a predominant religion in the far-east. In Buddhist temples, elephants are used for parades, processions, and other religious activities. The festivals in these temples are called Perahara. In Candy, this festival is conducted during the summer season. In this religious festival, a golden box containing the tooth of Lord Buddha is carried on the back of the elephant during the procession. Raja was the leader in those processions.

Candy used to be the capital of Sri Lanka. During the festival procession, more than fifty elephants followed the leading elephant that carried the gold box containing the tooth. There were occasions when the number following elephants exceeded one hundred. Elephants were decorated with strings of lights (serial bulbs) as we use for Christmas decorations. Even now, in some places in India, big torches are used in the processions ahead of the elephant convoy. At the Candy festival, they put dried coconut pieces (copra pieces) in metallic baskets containing burning coal or burning coconut shell. Raja lived in Candy between 1930 and 1988. There are so many interesting wide-spread stories about the tusker during that period.

People of Sri Lanka used to say respectfully that Raja was a "divine moving monument." In the year 1985, the president of Sri Lanka declared that Raja is the "treasure of the nation." Raja died in July of 1988 at a ripe old age of sixty-five. All the holy priests of the Buddhist religion paid their respect to the body of Raja, which was placed for viewing. Many people from various parts of the nation came to pay respect to Raja "lying in state." Because of the request of the priests of the Buddhist religion, his body was stuffed and kept in the national museum. In December of 1989, the national museum gave the life-size stuffed body of Raja to the "temple of tooth" for open public viewing. It still stands with the majestic look, like a raja, to receive the admiration and respect of his people.

Mahmud

The Christian calendar starts with the birth of Christ. The Islamic calendar starts from 622 AD. But unlike the Christian calendar, this is not related to the birth of the Prophet Mohammad. He was born fifty-two years earlier. This calendar is related to the emigration of the Prophet from Mecca to Medina. It is said that Muslims call it "year of the elephant." The story goes that a Christian Yemeni ruler attempted to conquer Mecca with a few war elephants. His intention was to destroy Kaaba, the central shrine in Mecca. Kaaba is predated to Islam. Islamic tradition claims that the elephant that let (commanded) the other war-elephants stopped moving forward at the border of Mecca and refused to proceed further for unknown reasons. Subsequently, the leader elephant was named prophetically Mahmud.

Charlemagne's elephant

Isaac was a wealthy Jewish trader. After his successful business tour of the Persian Empire and Africa, he returned to Europe and wanted to present an elephant to the Emperor. It was in 801 AD that his trip was sponsored by Charlemagne, the

Frankish king, who was the first Holy Roman Emperor. He wanted to procure an elephant from Haroun-al-Raschid, the Abbasid Caliph, and present it to the Emperor Charlemagne. Haroun and Charlemagne were friends. The elephant was named Abdul-Abbas, after the founder of Abbasid Empire. Charlemagne took this elephant to war when he fought with the Danes in the year 804 AD. One commendable thing that happened was the elephant steered clear of the fighting, even though European kings barely knew how to train elephants for war.

Elephant of Henry III

Henry was the King of England from 1207 to 1272. He received many gifts from several kings, including a camel from Frederic II, and a polar bear from the King of Norway. The exceptional gift, an African elephant, was from King Louis IX of France. He sent a letter to the Sheriff of London with an instruction to build "one house of forty feet long and twenty feet deep for our elephant." This animal of huge size was a feast to the eyes for Europeans and the visitors that poured in. Many artists drew sketches of the elephant, including Mathew Paris, the famous illustrator. Sadly enough, the elephant died after two years. The cause of death is said to have been the feeding of too much red wine!

Hanno: The Pope's pet

Tristan de Cunha was a Portuguese explorer. He led a grand procession to Rome in 1514 AD. The procession was really grand because it had an Indian white elephant, which was covered with gold brocade and silver safe-box with precious gifts. It was sent by King Manual I of Portugal as a gift to Pope Leo X. The elephant's name was Hanno. It was a tamed and trained elephant that knew and obeyed several commands. It knelt before the pontiff, who was very much impressed. It also sprayed trunkful of water to onlookers on command. This gift had a special purpose. The Portuguese king wanted claim to the newly discovered "spice island" to be approved by the Pope. These Spice Islands are the present- day Indonesia. It was the only source of mace and nutmeg in those days. The gift was well received and for several years Hanno appeared in several ceremonial functions of Rome. Unfortunately, Hanno died at a very young age of seven in 1516 AD. The pontiff requested the famous artist Raphael to paint a portrait of Hanno. But, unfortunately, this portrait is missing today. The Pope's critics made use of his love of elephants as heresy, since the animal presented Ganesh, a Hindu God. Even Martin Luther is said to have criticized the Pope on this account.

Elephant of Thomas Jefferson

Charles Wilson Peale was an American natural historian as well as a museum founder. He requested from Thomas Jefferson a grant to excavate the bones lying in a tar-pit near Newburgh, New York. Peale dug out a full skeleton of a North American mastodon in 1801 AD. Mastodons originated long before mammoths. They were not closely related but shared many common features. The mastodons and mammoths became extinct eleven thousand years ago. Elephants were descendants of mammoths and belonged to the same family, *Elephantidae*. Thomas Jefferson thought the skeleton Mr. Peale dug out was a mammoth. It was carefully mounted and displayed in a Philadelphia museum and was eleven feet tall. Jefferson thought mammoths were alive and still roaming in North America. He strongly believed that the skeleton was a mammoth. To clear up the doubt whether the skeleton was a mastodon or a mammoth, Jefferson requested Lewis and Clarke lead an expedition to collect more skeletons. William Clarke collected bones from Big Bone Lick, Kentucky, and sent them to Jefferson to clarify. Later, it was confirmed mammoths were extinct and the bones belonged to mastodons.

Lin Wang: National symbol of Taiwan

During World War II, the Japanese invaded Burma (Myanmar) and used logging-elephants of Myanmar to construct roads and bridges for the army. Chiang Kai-shek was smart enough to get thirteen of these elephants from the Japanese. They were marched to China along the Burma border but only seven of them survived until the end of the world war. These seven elephants were then utilized to build war memorials. Out of these, three were taken to Taiwan in 1947. Unfortunately only one elephant survived and was then given to Taipei City Zoo in 1954 AD as a gift. They named it Lin Wang, which means "forest king." It turned out to be a big crowd puller because of the history behind it. Lin Wang died at the ripe old age of eighty-six in 2003 and was made "Citizen of Taipei" posthumously.

Ahmed

Ahmed was a wild African elephant that was guarded by soldiers. Ahmed was one of the elephants that captured the attention of the whole world. He was probably the only wild elephant that received worldwide recognition while still alive. He was never captured. His name, Ahmed, means the "blessed one" in the Arabic language. He lived very close to the wildlife sanctuary Masha bid in Kenya, East Africa, sometime around the year 1910 AD. Ahmed was not an ordinary elephant. He was famous for his long tusks. On average, each tusk of an African male elephant weighs about thirty-two kilograms (70.4 pounds). However, Ahmed's tusks reached almost to the ground in his standing position and each tusk was three meters long and weighed sixty-eight kilograms (149.6 pounds). The weight of his tusk was more than double the average weight of an African elephant's tusk. His tusks still hold the world record.

Just after the Second World War, elephant killing for poaching tusks became rampant in Africa and this became a threat to Ahmed's life. There is no wonder that his pair of tusks, weighing 136 kilograms (299.2 pounds), attracted many poachers. This was a big concern for the animal lovers around the world and it prompted them to send letters (more than five thousand) to the wildlife sanctuary officials to take measures to protect Ahmed's life. These letters produced beneficial effects. A presidential order was issued to the military by Mr. Jomo Kenyatta, then president of Kenya, asking them to take appropriate measures to protect Ahmed's life by soldiers. Thus, the soldiers protected him throughout his life. Years later, on January 17, 1974, Ahmed passed away due to natural causes at an approximate age of sixty. At the time of his death he weighed approximately five tons. He was ten feet tall. They were not able to save Ahmed's skin for taxidermal purposes. However, Zimmermann, a taxidermy company, used fiberglass to make his figure, and his bones were taken to Nairobi, the capital of Kenya.

Tourists can still see Ahmed's skeleton and his life-size figure at the National Museum in Nairobi. In 1977, an elephant-loving group in Detroit chose Ahmed as the mascot of their organization. This move again boosted Ahmed to international fame in the modern world.

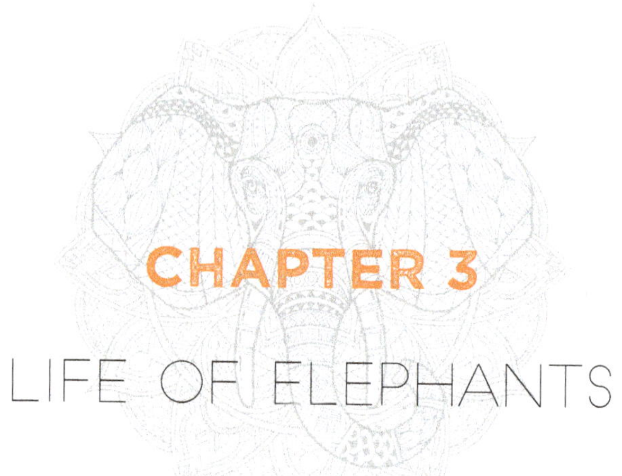

CHAPTER 3

LIFE OF ELEPHANTS

Reproduction in elephants

Elephants have a long gestation period of nineteen to twenty-one months. The intervals between births are also long. When women have long intervals between childbirth, it is jokingly called "elephant delivery." This type of "elephant delivery" became common in India when family planning was introduced to reduce population growth in the country. The central government had several family planning programs to control the population and a long interval between deliveries was one of the methods.

The location of the external genitalia in female elephants is low compared to that in other quadrupeds. Previously, people had several imaginary stories about mating in elephants, because it is a process that often occurred in the wild but rarely in captivity. However, in recent years people learned from TV programs that the mating process in elephants is similar to any other quadruped animals. The mating in elephants is also called "congress," which literally means a union. In the wild, female elephants reach reproductive stage between eleven and thirteen years of age. However, in captivity they get to this stage early because of good management practices, including balanced diets. The earliest record goes to a female Asian elephant that delivered at the age of five. Since gestation period is about two years, this elephant might have reached maturity at the age of three.

The estrous cycle in cow elephants lasts for about fourteen to seventeen weeks. The mating ritual in elephants has some peculiarities. The cow elephant and her lover (either a tusker or a tusk-less male called makhna) will move from the herd to a secluded place. Foreplay lasts for a long time, although the actual intercourse lasts only eight to forty-five seconds. After the first mating, they are able to mate again within thirty minutes to one hour. The couple will typically mate four to six time a day. They may continue this "mating friendship" for three to four days.

The newborn elephant baby will have an average weight of one hundred kilograms and a height one meter. Most of the time, the delivery takes place in the night. It does not take very long and the placenta is ejected within one to two hours. Although rare, twin babies have been reported.

Mother elephant with her twin babies

Within a short period of time, the newborn will find the nipple and start drinking milk. Elephants do not have teats like cows. Their mammary glands more closely resemble those of humans. The newborn calf may continue to feed on mother's milk for about three to four years. In captivity, this will interfere with the work schedule of the working mothers and the babies are weaned at about two years of age. Elephant mothers raised in captivity, such as in zoos, may hesitate to allow their newborns to suckle. In such cases the calves are bottle fed by humans, which has a lot of challenges. It is difficult to successfully hand-raise an elephant calf from birth.

In elephants, progesterone, an important hormone during the gestation period, is produced in low levels compared to other quadrupeds. It is measured in "picograms" (one millionth of a gram). A huge variation in the range of this hormone exists in elephants. To get a reliable assessment of the level of this hormone, it has to be measured at least a few times before gestation and continued for at least three months of pregnancy. The radioimmunoassay (RIA) kit that is used for testing the hormone in human beings can also be used in elephants with some success in case a specific elephant hormone kit is not readily available.

Artificial insemination has been successful in elephants, as in other animals. Mostly it is done in the Western world because of the difficulties in keeping male elephants in captivity for each herd. They have tried artificial insemination in two dozen elephants and half of the female elephants became pregnant and continued pregnancy to full term. Ultrasound scanning is also done in elephants, as in human beings, to check pregnancies. A special form of equipment has been designed just for elephants. In India, one such equipment is in Assam State. This equipment was brought to Kerala State recently to test some female elephants. In olden days, before the use of modern equipment, the movement of the fetus after thirteen or fourteen months of mating was used for pregnancy diagnosis. These fetal movements are clearly noticed when the elephants are taken to the ponds for giving baths. Elephant reproduction research started only fairly recently, approximately fifteen years ago. At that time it was mainly aimed to help various aspects of artificial insemination. For that reason, it was not given much attention or support by the local public, but the views are changing now.

Human-like characteristics in elephants

Elephants have emotions and are capable of expressing joy, anger, grief, compassion, and love. Their thought processing is complex and elephants can express deep feelings. They abundantly express their joy when they are with their loved ones, family members, and friends. They greet friends, especially when they are absent for some time, by lifting their trunks and they love to play games. Their excitement is beyond description when a new one is born in the herd. They bellow and blare during this occasion. Reunion of separated herd members is another enjoyable moment for them to celebrate. During this excitement period, a liquid oozes from their temporal glands located between the ears and eyes on each side. To show their affection, they rub each other, spin around, rumble, scream, and roar (trumpet). Urinating and defecating are also done.

A mother elephant often touches her baby with her trunk and legs to keep constant contact. When a calf is in danger, all members of the herd, along with the mother, come forward to protect the baby. Elephants also display their grief vividly. They remember and mourn over loved ones. They touch and smell remains of the dead ones and pay respect by standing still for some time. This is a kind of grieving process. Rage and stress are also expressed by elephants. They express a lot of rage when human-elephant conflict arises. They also suffer from chronic stress when their loved ones are killed and their habitat is lost. Human interference disrupts the delicate network of their family life. Their compassion is not only restricted to their loved ones but also to the other elephant herds and also to other animal species. There are reports that mothers sometimes carry their dead babies and the whole herd will move slowly to keep up with her.

A video that circulated on social media and captured everyone's attention some time ago showed a male baby elephant trying to revive his mother who was already dead. This happened near Kavidi Amman Kovil in Pallam, Coimbatore, Tamil Nadu State, India. According to the report of the wildlife department, the mother elephant was walking with the baby elephant when suddenly she fell down unconscious and died. The baby tried several ways to make his mother get up. He tried with his trunk to poke her face, and even got up on the mother to try to revive her. He continued this process for almost seven hours. He leaned on his mother's body and literally wept for an hour. When the forest officials came to remove him from the mother's body, he attacked them and continued his efforts to wake her up. Later, the divisional forest officer reported that it was really a difficult task to get the baby elephant separated from his mother. The officials sought help from a trained adult elephant to separate him from his mother. The veterinary doctor who performed the post mortem reported that the twenty-five-year-old mother elephant died of internal bleeding. The cause of the internal bleeding is not yet determined. This type of incident has occurred before in this town and officials are investigating further into this matter.

Elephant, a compassionate animal

The operation of the Dodpetta project was an eye opener in many aspects. This was a project to translocate elephants to another area. In order to do it, these elephants had to be tranquilized. During the operation, there were several incidents that show how much the elephants love each other. Dr. Cheeran, a team member of the project, was impressed and convinced of how much they value the love and affection among themselves.

There are several measures to be taken by the team members before they go to tranquilize an elephant in the wild. First of all, they all have to set their watches to the same time so they can note down the time of darting, time of antidote administration, and recovery time. There is no room for discrepancy in the records. Usually, the sharp shooter (darter) is the leader. He will be an expert in shooting and should be familiar with the forest and the elephants' behavior. He will start first. He is the one who shoots the dart syringe with the tranquilizer. He might have another individual as a partner to accompany him. The veterinary doctor will be on the back of a big and strong captive elephant. The rest of the team will be walking along with the captive elephant. Sometimes, the team that is following the sharp shooter may not be able to see him or hear the shot because when the elephant is sighted at a distance, the team stops. Only the darter goes near the elephant by "cat walk." He has to know the direction of the wind and according to the direction of the wind he may deviate from the path of the team to get closer to the elephant. The team behind him will not move closer to the elephant, but will be available in the vicinity. But when the animal is down, everybody has to reach the elephant as quickly as possible because the antidote has to be given immediately. Usually, the darter can see the animal very close and he has to inform the rest of the team when the elephant falls down. So, the understanding is that as soon as the elephant falls down he has to put a second shot (regular gun, no tranquilizer) in the air to inform the team behind him.

So on the day of tranquilization, everyone started in the early morning as previously planned. Around 10:30 in the morning everyone heard a shot. It was the first one they heard that morning. Everybody thought that it must be the tranquilizing shot. They used a shotgun rather than a rifle because this gun makes a bigger sound and can be heard with a distinct and distinguishing echo. This has another advantage:

When one elephant in a herd falls down, all other elephant won't run away from the scene as other animals do. They stay and try to help their fallen companion. Some in the herd will also try to attack the darter. This is an unusual behavior seen only in elephants. In other animals, such as deer, this behavior is not seen. When one is shot, all others will run away from the spot in all directions to save themselves.

As soon they heard the first shot, the team behind the darter quickly started rushing to the spot. As mentioned before, this team had captive elephants, veterinarians, and people to rope the fallen elephant. When the team was about to rush, there came another shot. Not one, but several of them for a minute or so. Everyone was stunned, suspicious that something went wrong. The elephant herd might have started attacking the shooter. In case an elephant comes towards you, the best way to stop it is to shoot, aiming for the front of the head (forehead) with a 12 bore gun. The impact will make a small dent in the forehead but nothing will happen to the elephant. It will not kill the animal. The elephant will be stunned for a few minutes (as if someone hit you on the head with a frying pan or a hammer). This will stop the elephant from advancing and gives you ample time to escape.

The team became completely confused. Nobody could figure out what was happening. Everyone was alert and readied their guns. The team as a whole started moving towards the spot from where the sound came. They saw that a tusker with an approximate age of thirty-five or forty years of age had fallen. They also saw several wounds on the front and sides of the head. It was clear that the wounds were skin deep.

When the real story came out from the darter, the team got the clear picture of the incident. When the tusker fell down, all other elephants in the herd were trying to raise his head to help him to get up. They tried this with their tusks, which caused the scoring wounds. The darter had to shoot continuously to the air in order to scare the other elephants to run away. These continuous shots were the ones that confused and scared the team.

Without wasting any time, the team members started their work. They put medicine to the wounds and fastened the elephant with ropes, and the captive elephants were asked to hold the ends of the ropes, then Dr, Cheeran himself administered the antidote to revive the elephant from unconsciousness (deep sedation). Thus, the fallen elephant got up in less than thirty minutes and was led by the captive elephant to the camp.

Other incidents of love and compassion

The female elephant Savithri and the male elephant Ravindran were very good friends and were also inseparable lovers. They were there for each other at all times. They were captive elephants living in Kerala State Forest Department, Kodanad Elephant Camp, Kerala State, India.

The end of their happy days together came suddenly, without warning. Ravindran got a respiratory infection and became ill. Thick phlegm started coming through his trunk. Dr. Krishna Murthy, a well-known veterinarian in Tamil Nadu, was brought in to treat Ravindran. When the condition did not improve as expected, another famous veterinarian, Dr. P.O. George, from Kerala Veterinary College, Mannuthy, was brought for a second opinion and accompanied by Dr. Cheeran. Still the condition of Ravindran did not improve and it went from bad to worse. Ravindran became so weak he could not stand up. Finally, he became "bedridden" and in order to prevent bedsores from developing, Ravindran had to be moved from one position to the other. Savithri and another captive elephant were used to help in this process. Although he got the best treatment available in those days, he finally succumbed to death. He was diagnosed with tuberculosis and in those days, specific medicines were not available for tuberculosis. The only medicine available was Streptomycin, which was discovered only a decade and half before the event, by Waksman and coworkers in 1944. Continuous treatment with this antibiotic was difficult even for humans. So, it goes without saying that treatment of the elephant with such large amounts of antibiotic was unthinkable, even by injection.

The authorities decided to do a post mortem of Ravindran's body. In order to do this, the body had to be pulled to another area far away from where he had died; Savithri and the other captive elephant helped the workers with this huge task. In order to bury the body after post mortem, the authorities dug a large ditch next to the area where the post mortem had been conducted. During the post mortem, Ravindran's thoracic and abdominal cavities were opened. Samples were collected for further histologic examination and other tests which confirmed the diagnosis of tuberculosis (TB). This was probably the first case of TB in elephants in Kerala State. Now there is a big project to screen and diagnose TB in elephants in the state.

The post mortem was conducted in open air. Although it was not a pleasant scene, a fairly large crowd of people showed up to watch. The other captive elephants were tied to trees nearby. The author did not notice Savithri in that group and later heard people saying that she showed some uneasiness about the procedures being done to Ravindran's body. After the postmortem was completed, the entire carcass had to be placed in the ditch and again they sought the assistance of the two elephants that had helped previously, including Savithri. Ropes were tied to the carcass and the ends of the rope were given to Savithri and the other elephant. The other elephant readily held the rope but to everyone's surprise, Savithri did not obey the command of the mahout. Savithri was an otherwise obedient captive elephant, and the officials were all taken aback. The mahout started forcing her to obey the commands using usual procedures, including beatings, but Savithri was adamant and wouldn't obey. Finally, everyone in the administration asked the mahouts to abandon the idea of getting help from Savithri. It was obvious that she could not bear the sight of Ravindran in this condition. Her intense suffering at witnessing this kind of torture to her friend and lover, Ravindran, was difficult, and without warning Savithri ran away. The surprised crowd was astonished that she quickly and with care avoided injury to them as she ran. And, as the crowd then gathered to bury Ravindran, it was clear they felt great sadness for her and appreciated her love for her friend. The people of the area still share fond memories of this event and love elephants have for one another.

Another incident refers to the predators of baby elephants. It is fair to say that elephants do not have any natural enemies in the animal kingdom except man. However, this statement is not true for baby elephants. When baby elephants are separated from the herd, they become vulnerable to attacks by carnivorous predators. In Africa, lions are the predators for baby elephants, whereas in India, tigers and leopards are the predominant predators.

Dr. Cheeran remembers an incident that took place in Chombey National Park in Botswana. One morning, a lioness was getting ready to attack an isolated baby elephant about fifteen meters away from her. She leaped quickly, without wasting a second, onto the baby elephant and thrust her sharp claws deep into the neck, causing the baby elephant to fall to the ground. The lioness bit the throat with her long and sharp canine teeth and killed the baby elephant instantly. Then, she began eating the flesh. As she finished her breakfast, three of her baby cubs came out of their hideouts in the bushes and took her place. Vultures, flying in the sky above the scene, suddenly came down and landed close to the cubs, ignoring their presence. The mother lioness attacked the vultures and kept them away. This process continued till late afternoon.

When it started getting dark, there appeared something resembling a "small hill." Within a few minutes, many more of these "small hills" started appeared. All were moving towards the remains of the dead baby elephant. The "small dark hills" were processions of elephants, with the oldest female in front of the procession. She could have been the grandmother of the baby elephant, as she looked very old. All gathered around the dead body of the baby elephant.

They started stomping on the ground, looking toward the direction the lioness and cubs had gone. They were making some sound, perhaps expressing their anger and grief, and they all touched and sniffed the dead body with their trunks, remaining silent for some moments.

Many more elephants came; probably more than one hundred elephants came within thirty-five or forty-five minutes. Everyone touched the dead body, squeezing through the crowd and retreating back. Within an hour, they all left in the same direction they had come from except one female elephant. She remained for some more time. According to the Botswanan guide, this female elephant must have been the mother of the baby elephant. She smelled the baby's body and walked to the spot where the baby was actually killed. She urinated and defecated on that spot. Then she stomped on the ground with her front legs and splashed dirt all around the area. Then she turned to the area where the lioness and her cubs had been hiding, lifted her trunk to get the scent and left. It was obvious that she had tremendous feelings. Could it be the frustration, sadness, anger, or a combination of all these emotions? She did not bother the remains of the dead body anymore, perhaps thinking she'd let those "devils" finish the rest of the body. She walked straight to the place where she came from without turning back, not even once. She soon joined the rest of the elephants who had attended "the funeral" and the group continued moving forward silently. For Dr. Cheeran, this raised some questions: Was this a memorial service, or a routine funeral service, for the dead among elephants? Do elephants have emotions and sorrows? Do they express their compassion and sorrow like human beings, or even more so?

Do elephants cry?

A male captive elephant with one tusk (instead of a pair) once escaped from a wood-logging camp to a nearby forest in Sholayar, a place in Kerala State, India. Usually, elephants run to the forest when they don't like the current environment or when they are in musth. When they do, elephants can be unfriendly and more likely dangerous. Dr. Cheeran and his partner were contacted when the elephant escaped to the forest. So, they, along with their associates, had to go catch the elephant by tranquilization. It was an adventurous event that lasted for three or four days.

In order to find the escaped elephant, the team did a "noisy search" inside the forest. At this time, an elephant showed up from within the forest. There were a lot of big logs piled up on the banks of a river. There was also a truck parked to load the logs. When the elephant showed up, Dr. Cheeran and his partner thought it was the same dangerous elephant that was lost. Since the elephant had two tusks, they immediately knew it must be another elephant, not the one they were looking for. The mahout, who was with the team, suspected that this elephant was a captive one and not a wild one. He slowly approached the elephant, taking all the precautions possible because it could be a wild elephant and in that case the mahout's like would be in danger. He carefully started giving commands in a loud voice from a distance.

The elephant began to obey his commands and he gradually led the elephant to a nearby police station. Later he tethered the elephant with chain to a tall tree there. Then they came to know that one month before the incident, there was one elephant that was brought to that area for timber logging and was stationed there. One day he got loose and escaped to the forest. At that time an intense search was conducted but all efforts were in vain. They could not find the elephant. The owner of the elephant was exhausted both in money and patience and finally abandoned the search and went home. It is worth mentioning at this point that the owner had received the elephant as a part of his dowry.

After more inquiries into this incident, they were able to get some more information about the elephant. He had escaped to the forest because the mahout stabbed him during the timber logging work. They were able to see a one-month-old stab wound in the inner thigh region of the elephant. With the help of police, the owner was informed about the return of his elephant. The very next day the owner came. The meeting of the owner and the elephant was very emotional. The owner held the trunk of the elephant and started crying and saying, "Oh my son, why did you run away from me?" To everyone's surprise, the elephant also started crying. The tears were flowing profusely. So, elephants have emotions like people. A similar experience was also narrated by the author's veterinarian friend, Dr. Pushkaran.

Now let us look at the scientific aspect of flowing of tears. There are no tear glands in elephants. Tear gland exists in all other known mammals. Although elephants are mammals, instead of tear glands they have Harderian glands, which are also seen in birds. This is important biologically and it is a mystery why elephants have Harderian glands like birds. These glands are not seen in any other mammals.

Another interesting thing is that almost all mammals have a duct that connects the eyes and the nose, so when they are sad, tears start flowing through the nose as well as the eyes, as in people. Rhinorrhea (profuse flowing of tears) is a common sign when someone cries. This duct is absent in elephants. So, all tears come only from the eyes which we perceive as profuse flow of tears.

It is easy to show that elephants produce tears, but it is not possible to demonstrate these tears from emotions; however, based on circumstance and behavioral pattern, we can assess whether or not it is due to emotions. For example, at the time of death of a baby elephant, the herd, particularly the mother elephant, stays with the dead baby and grieves for a long time with water in her eyes.

Elephant babies are happy when grandmas are with them

Elephant herds are just like human families. Babies and grandparents are always buddies when it comes to people. This is absolutely true for elephant families too. We all know that however strict parents might be to their kids, they will be very lenient towards their grandchildren. When they are with babies, they also behave like babies. A study conducted in Cambodian elephants revealed this is absolutely true for elephants. When the scientists investigated the social life of elephants it was clear that their social life is very similar to humans. The study also revealed that the baby elephant living with grandma elephants live longer and their survival rate is much better than those who don't have grandmas in the herd. The survival rate is almost eight fold when babies have grandmas with them. These grandmas not only take care of the grand-calves but also train the mothers how to take care of their babies. They are the leaders in the herd. They help the members to find sources of water, safe places, and food. They protect the babies, keep track of them and rescue them when they get stuck in the mud. They also help the members to interact with members of other herds. Elephants, people, non-human primates, and some whales live longer, even after their reproductive period of life. In other animals, many of them do not get an opportunity to see their grandbabies. Even if they do see them, no bond has been observed among grandmas and grandbabies. For scientists it has raised the question as to why elephants live such long lives if they are not reproducing offspring. Apparently, their purpose is to care for their grandbabies while their daughters are actively reproducing, thus improving the survival rate of the species. One other supporting fact is that baby elephants born in captivity (zoos) have a 50 percent lower survival rate, even with good care from their mothers. This strongly suggests the importance of social life in elephants and the role of grandmothers. One study performed by students of the University of Norway reported that grandmas assist young female elephants in finding suitable "grooms" for mating. Grandma elephants only give this training to their daughters.

Elephant, a great swimmer

Can elephants swim? It is an eyebrow-raising question for those who are not associated with elephants. They must be wondering how such a huge animal like an elephant can swim. There are many instances when an elephant has gotten into a pond and did not want to come back out. Once, when the elephant did not want to come back to land, people brought a buffalo, and the elephant got scared and came back to the land. Another time, they burned tire like a torch to scare the elephant and that worked. Sometimes the problem is the people who gather around to see the activities of the elephant. An incident that occurred in Muvattupuzha, Kerala State, India, is a typical example. One elephant got into the river. Dr. Cheeran and his team went to get the elephant back to the banks of the river. It was in the day time. A lot of people gathered on both banks of the river to see the elephant's activities. They gathered not only on the banks of the river, but also on a bridge that was across the river. Every time the elephant swam close to the bank, people screamed with joy and the elephant would go back to the water (to the middle of the river) again. Finally, the team intentionally misguided the people by telling them that they would use a tranquilizer the next day and hoist the elephant using a crane and bring him back to land. After saying this, the team left the location, and so did the people. A few hours later, in the early morning hours (around three a.m.), the team went to the area with bananas and jackfruit, and called the elephant, which swam back to the river bank.

There are several reports that elephants swam several hours continuously without touching the ground. In Andaman Islands (Indian Territory) in Bay of Bengal, elephants swim continuously for hours from one island to the other. This swimming was broadcasted on various channels of televisions. When they swim to cross rivers with baby elephants, the strongest and largest one in the herd will be the one first to face the flow of water (upstream). On the babies' side (downstream) will be the comparatively smaller elephant, so the babies are in between. In captive elephants, the mahouts will stand on the top of the elephants when they swim across big rivers. Sometimes, elephants try to take a dip during the swim and mahouts standing on the top will not get wet completely in a standing position.

Elephants breathe through their trunk; therefore, the trunks lift up. This is more or less like snorkeling, with the elephant's trunk acting as a snorkel. Biologically there is an explanation for all these activities. Elephants' origin is from water and there are some body peculiarities they share with whales that prove this concept. For example, whales are marine mammals; buoyancy helps them keep afloat to move around in water. Another peculiarity which whales share with elephants is that the testicles are located inside the body. The temperature of the testicles has to be below their body temperature. The blood circulation of the testicles is very different from the general blood circulation to keep them at lower temperature. Their hemoglobin, which stores oxygen, is capable of keeping the oxygen as oxyhemoglobin for a very long time. The hemoglobin of elephants and that of whales are similar. More points, such as the absence of pleura that cover the lungs, lack of sweat glands, and control of temperature through ears, lend to support their origin from water. However, the opponents of this theory insist that none of these points are essential for a species to have origins from water. Once, Dr. Cheeran was chatting with an official of the National Swiss Circus, a famous circus company in Switzerland, and was told an interesting story of an elephant. The company has some excellent elephants. When they were taken for a bath in Geneva Lake, one elephant actually swam all the way to the other side of the lake, which was in the mainland of France. Dr. Cheeran was amused by the thought that animals do not need a passport or visa

Elephants volunteer to their cemetery?

Some tribal people in Africa believe that when an elephant is about to die, it will move from the rest of the herd to a specific lonely place and will lie down there waiting for death to come. Such isolated places become a sort of cemetery for elephants. The average life span of an elephant is sixty years. At the age of forty years, the final molar teeth in the upper and lower jaw on either side will replace the old ones. These four molar teeth will eventually be worn out by the time the elephant reaches sixty years of age. Once they are worn out, the elephant cannot eat roughage consisting of leaves and other fibrous material. In the wild, they get only these types of roughage. So, they face death due to starvation. In captivity they get cooked food such as rice and other gruel. Consequently, they can live ten to fifteen years longer in captivity.

Scientists do not approve the tribal people's concept of cemetery. The supporting evidence for the cemetery concept is that the bones and sometimes the whole skeleton of elephants are seen in piles in specific places. The proponents of the concept believe that the elephants nearing death assemble in a lonely place, seeking their end. Before we discuss the cemetery concept any further, we should understand their behavior and habitat.

There are more African elephants in the savanna grass meadows than Asian elephants in the thick forests of Asia.

It is said that elephants that are seen in the west of Namibia drink water only once every two days. The main reason for this is the availability of food, which is often far away from the water source. For food and water, they have to travel long distances. Elephants in general have the ability to walk long distances and, in fact, if they don't walk, they get foot problems. When elephants get old, they try to settle in places where they can get food and water within a short walking distance. When the old elephants camp in a convenient place where food and water are available, such places will often look like "old folks' homes." This may explain why piles of bones are seen in some specific places.

Another possibility is that hunters hide in places where elephant traffic is heavy. Hunters kill them in large numbers to take tusks for ivory and leave the bodies there to decay. This could be the reason for seeing large heaps of bone in one particular area. A third possibility is that surviving elephants gather bones of the dead ones. There are some elephant scientists who believe that the bones of dead elephants are revered by the remaining relatives in the herd. They pick up the bones and bring them to a specific place as a ritual. This could be another reason for seeing large heaps of elephant bones.

In thick forests of Asia, the dead body of an elephant won't stay in a place for very long. Other wild animals such as hyenas, foxes, and birds, such as vultures, eat and clear the flesh and internal organs. The animals such as porcupines are good at scavenging bones. So, heaps of bone are a rare sight in Asian forests.

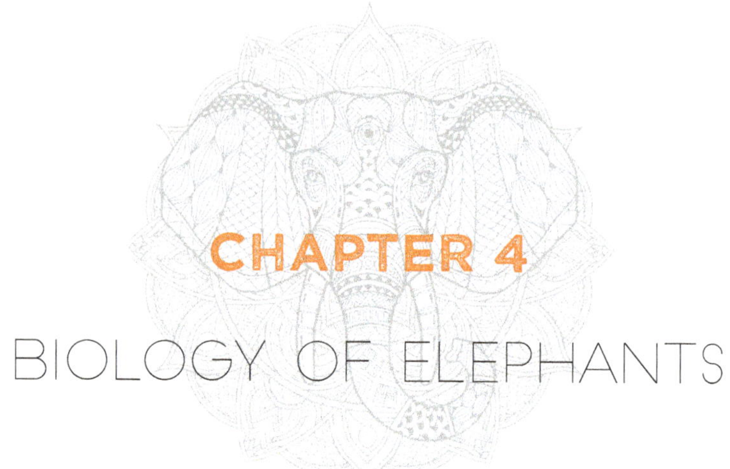

CHAPTER 4

BIOLOGY OF ELEPHANTS

Elephant's trunk

THE ELEPHANT TRUNK IS a unique organ with many purposes. From an evolutionary and anatomic standpoint, the trunk is formed by the union of nose and the upper lip. African elephants have two finger-like projections at the tip of the trunk, whereas Indian elephants have only one finger-like projection. According to scientists, the trunk is made up of more than one hundred thousand muscles. These muscles help to manipulate the trunk for various functions, such as carrying huge logs of wood or even picking up small leaves from the ground.

Most herbivores use their teeth to eat, biting and tearing apart leaves and small plants. Baby elephants also do this. However, adult elephants use their trunks to hold and tear branches from trees and use their teeth only for chewing. If the fruit on the tree are too high to reach, an elephant will try to shake the tree by holding its trunk around the tree. Sometimes, it will try to knock down the tree. It can stand on its hind legs, lift up the forelimbs, and stretch the trunk to reach fruits or a branch of a tree.

Elephants use their trunks to drink water; they can suck water through the trunk and pour it into the mouth. When they are in the river or pond, they use their trunks the same way to splash water onto the backs of their bodies. Even after a nice bath, they might put mud and dirt on their bodies, using their trunks in order to escape the intense heat of the sun. In fact, sometimes they cover their entire bodies with dirt to keep cool and control body temperature. In addition, they use their trunks to greet each other or greet humans in ceremonies. Trunks are also used to smell specific odors of predators, such as lions and people. Elephants can raise the trunk high in the air and wave it to find the location of food, friends, and enemies by smell.

How many teeth for an elephant?

In Sanskrit language, one of the oldest languages in the world, *dantha* means tooth. Elephants are also called *danthi*. So, how many *danthas* are there for a *danthi*? The origin of the name *danthi* probably came from the fact that the incisor teeth are transformed into tusks in elephants. Usually among the domestic animals, cattle and goats have sixteen teeth each, pigs have twenty-two, dogs have twenty-three, and cats have fifteen teeth. Horses have nineteen teeth but in mares the canine teeth do not erupt. Another interesting thing in ruminants (cattle and goats) is that there are no incisors present in the upper jaw.

In an elephant there is only a pair of molars in both the upper and lower jaws, with a total of four teeth at a time. The deficiency in their count is compensated by the size of the tooth. As you know, the elephant's mouth is very small compared to its body size. In a fully grown adult elephant each molar is the size of a brick. In addition, there is a peculiarity in the way a new tooth replaces the old one. In all domestic animals, tooth eruption occurs twice in their lifetime, as in human beings. In the case of elephants, it occurs six times in their life. The first eruption (replacement) occurs when they are four months old, then in the sixth month, then at three years, then at six years, then at twenty years, and the final replacement at forty years. The last replaced teeth last for about twenty years without any significant wear and tear. However, after sixty years of age, the last tooth wears down faster and will soon be lost. At that point, they cannot chew rough vegetation properly and their health deteriorates very fast and they succumb to death quickly. This situation is common in the wild. However, in captivity they are given cooked food such as rice and they lead a fairly good life for ten or more years with proper care and management.

Usually, an animal's age is determined by checking the condition of teeth. This concept may be the basis for the famous saying, "Don't look a gift horse in the mouth". Mostly this applies to cows or horses. The age of an elephant can also be determined by checking its teeth. The only problem is, when you check the teeth you have to figure out how many eruptions have occurred earlier in that animal. This can be determined by looking at the ridges on the surface of the molar. At each replacement the ridges on the surface of the tooth varies. The number of ridges increases as the replacement progresses. Usually this method is difficult because the elephant won't keep its mouth open long enough for you to finish counting the ridges. Another problem is that the elephants cannot extend the tongue as we do. Since they don't open the mouth long enough to finish counting ridges, the best way is to take a photograph of the surface quickly when the mouth is opened, then to count the ridges by examining the photograph. Another way is to make the elephant bite on hard dough and peel it off from the tooth and count the ridges. However, these methods are not practical in a live elephant. In a deceased animal, counting the ridges on the surface of the tooth is a fairly accurate method of determining the age of the elephant.

Another interesting thing in the dentition of the elephant is that the replacement of the tooth does not occur the way we see in human beings. The teeth are not erupted either from the upper or lower jaws. The new tooth comes from behind (back of the jaw) as the current tooth gets worn out. Finally, the new one occupies the same position of the current one. The worn-out tooth falls off and is often mistaken for a broken tooth. Sometimes it is quite possible to see a new and an old tooth at the same time just before the old one falls out.

How big is an elephant's head?

In Malayalam, a regional language in India, "Ana Thala" means elephant head. This is the literal meaning. The term elephant head in another sense denotes "large size" of the object. In an old song that praises Lord Krishna, a devotee sings that he will give a pile of butter the size of an elephant head as an offering to please the Lord. Lord Krishna is well-known for his love of butter. In this context, elephant head means a large quantity. Now the question is: Does it mean the elephant has a large brain? The answer is that its brain does not occupy the entire head. There are several pockets of empty space inside the head called sinuses and so the brain only occupies a small percentage of the size of the head. However, there are several descriptions and stories indicating the wisdom and intelligence of elephants. How to evaluate the intelligence of an animal is a mindboggling question. Scientifically, the evaluations are based on the history of the evolution of the brain, expansion of behavioral patterns, life of the animal in a herd, and its ability to solve maze tests or puzzles, etc. Let us share some of the studies scientists did to compare the intelligence of elephants with other animals.

It is an undisputed statement that human beings, which fall under the "primates" classification of the animal kingdom, are the most intelligent animal in the world. Our ability to develop language to express ourselves and communicate with each other is considered the hallmark of our intelligence. Our ability to transfer this knowledge to the next generation is supporting this contention that we are the most intelligent species on this planet. Among the other animals, non-human primates like chimpanzees, sea animals like dolphins, and the largest land animals, elephants, are generally considered very intelligent animals.

It is now well accepted that the size of the brain is not the only "yard stick" for measuring intelligence. For example, dogs and crows have fairly small brains but their intelligence is well recognized and proven. Scientists have not reached a common consensus to approve the standard measure for evaluating intelligence. Each species overcomes their complex life-situation differently. However, whatever the complex situation and whatever the method used to measure, if the test subjects are successful it clearly shows their ability and intelligence.

The total size of the brain may be an indication of intelligence in most animals. However, this cannot be applied to all animals. For example, the average weight of brain of domestic animals such as cows, horses, and camels is 560-760 grams, whereas chimpanzees have only 330-430 grams. Therefore, scientists came up with a consensus that rather than taking the absolute weight of the brain, it is better to take the ratio of brain weight to the body weight. When they did more experiments with this concept they realized that it is not only the brain, but also the entire nervous system, including the number of neurons, neural connections, their size, and the distance from the organ to the brain that are all involved in the final manifestation of intelligence and wisdom.

The following table depicts intelligence quotients of various animals based on the weight of the brain, number of neurons, and their connections. Please note that humans have the highest intelligence quotient and chimpanzees come next to humans.

Animal	Weight of brain in grams	Neurons in the system	Intelligence Quotient

Whale	2600-9000	1050	1.8
African Elephant	4200	1150	1.3
Human Being	1250-1450	580	2.8
Gorilla	430-570	430	1.5-1.8
Chimpanzee	330-430	620	2.2-2.5

***Indian elephants are considered more intelligent than African elephants. Indian elephants have an intelligence quotient of 2.**

The longest tusk unearthed

Mastodons are not closely related to elephants, but they share many common features with mammoths, which are comparatively recent ancestors of elephants. Recently, one of the tusks of this extinct animal (mastodon) was unearthed in two places in Greece at different times. One of these was discovered in Melia, a place 430 kilometers from Athens. This tusk had a length of 4.6 meters. It had growth rings which enabled the scientists to determine changes in the weather in that era. Mastodons were similar to mammoths but did not have curvy tusks.

Although mastodons had been extinct in Europe and Asia for almost two million years, they were still believed to be living in North America until ten thousand years ago. It is estimated that the tusk that was discovered in Greece was almost 205 million years old. These animals had a height of 3.5 meters and a life-span of fifty-five years. Scientists have also discovered a complete skeleton of a mastodon and estimated the age of the animal at the time of death as twenty-five to thirty years, height 3.5 meters and weight six tons.

Scientists are trying to isolate DNA from these tusks. Recently scientists were able to isolate DNA from a

130,000-year-old tusk that was discovered in Alaska. Several tusks were discovered later in Melia, Greece. A crane operator accidently discovered a five-meter-long tusk. Fifteen years ago, excavators further discovered a tusk measuring 4.39 meters long. In recent times, several skeletal parts of the mastodon have been found by excavators in Greece.

Another discovery was a skeleton of a prehistoric elephant which lived more than a million years ago. This was from Stavros, Russia. The laborers working in the field discovered this skeleton in an open pit. This is the fourth skeleton of a prehistoric elephant discovered in the world so far. The skeleton itself had a height of four meters (thirteen feet) and a length of six meters. Now, when we evaluate the size of an elephant, ten feet height is considered to be a big tall elephant. If the skeleton of an elephant itself is thirteen feet tall, then you can imagine the size of the elephant when it was alive. No question that they must have been larger than the present-day elephants.

CHAPTER 5

TALENTS OF ELEPHANTS

Elephant, the artist

Can an elephant draw a picture? How important is this question to those who are associated with art? How do they value this ability in elephants? Scientists performed some interesting experiments with elephants.They taught elephants how to hold a brush in their trunks. According to them, this task is one of the most frustrating jobs in the world. Most of the elephants will try to bite it or throw away. However, by repeated positive rewards such as fruits and sugarcane sticks, the scientists were finally able to succeed.

Later, they taught elephants how to hold a brush dipped in different colors of paints. The next step was to train them to draw on paper stuck to a wall. When they tried it for a few weeks, elephants were able to draw something on a sheet of paper kept on the ground or on an easel. If the elephant and the trainer have a good relationship, the elephant will comply with the trainer, drawing good artistic pictures using different colors of paint. In Thailand they use elephants to draw pictures. Sometimes, many elephant-drawn pictures are auctioned at a good price. At a fundraising function after the great tsunami, one such picture was sold at a high price of US $39,000 in 2005.

At the end of an exhibition conducted by the Elephant Study Center in Lampung, Thailand, there was a demonstration of elephants' talent in drawing. Most of the elephant-drawn pictures were auctioned. Dr. Cheeran, being a guest, also received a picture as a gift. Recently, Ms. Barbara, an American lady, trained a baby elephant in Kerala to draw pictures. As a fashion designer, she is incorporating these pictures commercially into fabrics, which are getting good demand in markets. She promises a good percent of the profit will go to elephant welfare.

The largest picture ever drawn by an elephant is in Thailand. It was shown by AXN channel in the TV show "Ripley's World of Guinness Records." Some of the captions on these drawings were "Cold Wind," "Gaze Ling Mist," and "Charming Lana." The names of the elephant artists were Congun, Van Pen, Kamsan, Lankan, Duvan Pun, Song Pun, Pan Pettus, and Pu Das. Pictures were drawn using eight panels and it took six hours to draw each one. After every hour a break of twelve to twenty minutes was given to the elephants. Each picture is 2.4 meters in width and twelve meters in length. This was conducted at the Maesa Elephant Center in Thailand.

Exploring the artistic talent of elephants is wonderful but there are some people who believe that in order to make the elephant an artist it requires torturing methods in the training process. They say that inside the tip of the trunk elephants have very sensitive nerve endings and keeping the brush is very painful for animals. In order to obey the command of the trainers, they use nails and sharp objects to induce pain. A concern was raised by animal activists and they wanted the tourists to boycott this kind of demonstrations and shows. As a result of protests, Measa Elephant Center publicly announced that they do not use any torturing methods to train elephants.

They said they use positive rewarding methods for elephants to obey commands.

Elephants can hear through their feet

Scientific investigations have proved that elephants have the ability to hear low volume sounds (infrasonic sounds) which can't be heard by many other animals or man. The lead for this research came from the book *Silent Thunder* by Katherine Payne, an author and a scientist in her own right. Scientists have already shown that sound and light are differentiated neither by ears nor eyes; instead, these signals bring only the information to the specific centers in the brain which make the differentiation. There is a common expression among scientists: "Hear the lightening and see the thunder." It is said that if the nerves from these organs are surgically interchanged, theoretically it is possible to hear the lightening and see the thunder.

For a long time, researchers have understood that the feet of elephants can act as a hearing organ. The sound waves in this type of communication travel within the surface of ground rather than in the air. Communication can be heard two ways. One, by ordinary soundwaves through air and the other by vibrations transmitted through ground. An extensive study lasting for twelve years was carried out in Etosha National Park in Namibia in western Africa. The research started in 1992 and ended in 2004. The results of this study were compiled and published in the book *The Secret Organ of Elephants: The Unknown Areas of African Wild Elephant Herds* by Caitlin O'Connell. The soundwaves through ground travel a greater distance than those through air, which dissipates faster. Elephants can communicate long distances (more than thirteen miles) through ground, with low frequency waves.

The scientists were actually investigating the damage caused by elephants in agriculture fields when they observed an unusual behavioral pattern in them. In order to hear usual sounds, elephants will concentrate with ears perked and swinging back and forth. However, in order to hear a sound coming from a distance, the herd will stand still, leaning forward and pressing forelegs to the ground. Sometimes, they lift one foreleg and hold it in that position. The most interesting thing is that all the elephants in the herd do the same thing at the same time. In other words, it was not a coincidental activity. They did this activity when other elephant herds came towards them or a jeep passed by them. Although this ability has been shown in small animals like rats and arachnids, scientists never expected that large mammals like elephants would have such a capability. In order to determine that elephants could recognize waves, they adopted a measure to test this. They used a sound developer (machine that can produce sounds at different wave lengths) and when elephants identified this wave, they rewarded them with treats such as fruits, cane sugar sticks, and apples as a positive reinforcement. If they could not recognize it, they were told repeatedly they were wrong or incorrect. To hear the terms "wrong" and "incorrect" was frustrating for the elephants.

The vibrations are sensed by the elephant with its toes, which have acoustically sensitive fat pads behind them. Similar tissue has been identified in their trunks also. Vibration signals are carried along the bones to the elephant's middle ear. Just like regular sound, the incoming signals are processed in the auditory cortex of the brain. Elephants can decipher the meaning of this low frequency transmission and can identify the source, such as an enemy or friend, or something natural, such as rain or earthquake. They also communicate with each other through this system. They give warning signals to members of the herd to take precautionary measures or to spread good news about rain and water availability.

Speed walking in elephants

Elephants are the largest land mammals. Many people think that since elephants are big, they are good sprinters for short distance and can run very fast. In reality, they cannot run. The truth is that they can do only a speed walk. Their inability to run is due to the unusual anatomy of their legs.

Scientists have conducted several investigations with regard to elephants' movements. The range of their speed is fourteen kilometers to thirty-six kilometers per hour. Some claim that when they charge an object, their speed at that moment can reach 120 kilometers. This is only for a very short period of time (a few seconds or fraction of a minute). However, more accurate scientific studies were conducted and the results have shown that elephants can move at a maximum speed of 24.5 kilometers per hour. For this study, they used zoo elephants in Europe and America during a competitive race. They also used Asian elephants from Thailand, which are trained to play polo. This study was continued with fourteen African elephants and forty-eight Asian elephants. The scientists used elephants with body weight ranging from 116 kilograms (young elephants) to large adult ones weighing 4,632 kilograms. They incorporated 2,400 steps of each animal in the data analysis.

Elephant race

In order to study elephants' body movements, scientists took a video of their "running" after putting large white paint dots on different parts of the body, such as the back of their neck, front of the head, forelegs, and rear legs. After the race, these videos were analyzed with the help of computers. They also compared elephants' slow walk without any haste and their fast walk (so-called running) at maximum speeds. They concluded that on average, an elephant can normally walk at a speed of fourteen kilometers per hour. They can also go at a maximum speed of 24.5 kilometers per hour. However, when elephants are transported from one location to another by walking, they walk at an average speed of 4.5 kilometers per hour.

Mirror, mirror, on the wall...

There are only a few animals in the world that can recognize their reflection on the mirror as their own image. These animals are chimpanzees and dolphins. This ability includes them in the category of intelligent animals. Research experiments have shown recently that elephants can also be included in this category. Most animals and birds will attack when they see their reflection in the mirror. The readers might have seen birds getting aggressive when they see their images in the mirror or in windows. It is because they cannot distinguish that these reflections are their own images. But elephants' reactions to their images are different. They don't try to attack the images. This ability distinguishes them from most other animals and provides evidence for their higher intelligence.

The scientific community had already approved the personality of "self-confidence" and "sacrifice" in elephants long before they recognized elephants' ability to identify their own images in the mirror. Until recently, the scientific community believed that only chimpanzees and dolphins could recognize reflections in a mirror as their own. The following research experiments confirmed those misbeliefs.

The famous experiments were conducted in the Bronx Zoo, New York. They utilized Indian elephants for these experiments. They installed a big mirror in an empty space in the elephant pen. Scientists used a 2.5-square-meter mirror, which could reflect the entire body of the elephant when they walked along. First, they made the mirror elephant- proof. Elephants usually attack by hitting an opponent using the front of their heads, piercing with their tusks, and also using their trunks in various ways. The scientists did not use a glass mirror—they used a plastic mirror so that the elephants would not break it. This mirror was made to withstand all types of attacking activities and, using an iron frame for this plastic mirror, they bolted it to the wall. Still the researchers were not entirely confident of the preparation. They were expecting the unexpected. Anything could happen at any time. However, to their surprise, the elephants did not attack but were curious to see their own reflections in the mirror.

The first thing the elephants did was search for something behind the mirror. Later, they knew that there was nothing but the wall. Some even wanted to search behind the wall. Some of them knelt on their knees to search for the animal behind the mirror. Although these types of experiments were done previously, at that time the mirrors were placed far away from the elephants. The mirrors were also very small, so the elephants could not perform these types of curious activities. In this experiment, they were able to satisfy their curiosity to know more about their reflection.

Elephants, when they see other friendly elephants, perform some activities that indicate their friendliness. These include mutual holding of trunks and gentle rubbing of heads on each other. This indicates they have become friends or they are renewing their old friendship. In the above-mentioned experiment, when they realized that there was no other elephant behind the mirror, they recognized it was their own image. At that point, their actions became very different. They wanted to test their own activities by touching their bodies with their own trunks or putting the tips of their trunks in their mouths while looking at the mirror and watching their activities more than their image. It seemed they were more amused and curious by their own activities, rather than the reflection of the image itself.

There was a final test, which an elephant named Happy passed with flying colors. Scientists put a brightly colored "X" mark on her forehead; Happy recognized that mark in the reflection. When they put the same mark without color, she did not recognize it at all. Even in chimpanzees, which are considered more intelligent, only 50 percent will be successful in this test. For elephants, throwing dirt and sand onto the body to cool down (learned habits), and identifying and recognizing the "X" mark is an excellent feat that provides proof of high intelligence.

The scientists are also planning to test the age at which they develop the ability to recognize reflections. In human babies, this ability develops when they are about eighteen months of age. We can hope that new information will come after the results of study. In the Western world, since there is a shortage of elephants at various young ages, it would be difficult to get a statistically sound number to do such experiments. Let us hope for the best. Eventually we will be able to get new information.

Elephants digging wells

It amazes a lot of people when they hear that elephants dig wells. Along with the amazement, several questions, such as where, how, how deep, and why also pop up.

The African continent is the place where you see several herds of elephants at a time. Most rivers in this continent dry up during the summer time. Although African elephants don't crave for water like Asian elephants, water for drinking is a must for all animals. An elephant can take four to eight liters of water in its trunk at a time. The daily requirement of water for an elephant is 150 to two hundred liters. Elephants seen in drought regions such as Namibia might drink their daily requirement of 150 to two hundred in one-stretch. Asian elephants, on the contrary, drink water frequently in small portions. In captive conditions, they can be trained to drink water only twice a day.

In dried up rivers, elephants will start digging to get water. You might have heard about some people who have special talents identifying the spot for digging wells, often called "water diviners." So, it goes without saying that identifying the spot to dig is an important matter. Some people say that elephants get the knowledge by natural instinct or that it is transferred from generation to generation. Scientific analysis shows that they have special features in their feet to help them to identify the spots accurately.

Elephants can sense minute vibration of the ground through their foot. When they walk on a dry floor of the river, they are able to identify a spot underneath where water is stored. Careful observation of these animals has revealed that their first step in digging is to identify the spot. In order to identify the spot they walk slowly and gently on the dry ground. When one elephant in the herd identifies the spot, others walk to the place where he identified the spot and test by walking there to approve it. The next step is to make the ground loose by thrusting. The loose soil is then removed to a distant area with their trunks. They continue to do this till water appears. When water starts coming, the workers drink water first and let others in the herd drink next. They leave when everyone in the herd has quenched their thirst. When the herd leaves, other small wild animals come and share the water.

You wonder how magnificent Mother Nature is!

Some peculiarities of elephants

Everyone knows that the elephant is an interesting animal. An individual can spend hours watching an elephant and its behavior. This may be the reason why elephants have become an integral part of zoos. Generally, it is very expensive to keep elephants in zoos. They need special buildings and careful maintenance practices, and these expenses are exhaustive.

Old Hindu religious books and popular folk stories deal with extensive descriptions of elephants. In Hindu mythology, Devendra, the king of Devas in heaven, used an elephant named Iravatham as his vehicle. *Kumara Sambhavam* is an old epic by the famous poet Kalidasa, who recognized the importance of elephants in the community and gave an elegant description of them in his book.

Elephants have an amazing ability to imitate sounds. Elephants that are kept near the railway stations imitate the sound of trains. Elephants that are kept near the farm areas in Kerala, India, can imitate water buffalo sounds.

The elephant's walk is another peculiarity. Their toes are interconnected with thick muscle fibers. This helps them to walk either on hard surface or marshy lands without slipping, and to keep the same pace of walk. There are some peculiarities in the process of lying down also. They will try to avoid it, even if they are very tired. It is very difficult for an adult elephant to get up from the recumbent position. Again, because of this, they hesitate to assume this position in a strange place. Therefore, an elephant in a lying position is a rare scene for many people. They cannot lie down for a long time with their chest facing down (ventral position). In olden days, before the use of glucose in treatments, an elephant in a lying down position indicated the end of the animal's life. This could be the reason in the Malayalam language the term *cherinju*, which means lay down, is used to denote the death of elephants.

Elephants are pretty good at long-distance walking. They might have gotten this capability to meet their requirement of large amounts of food (fodder). They require food equal to the amount of 5 percent of their body weight per day. They eat one hundred and fifty to two hundred and fifty kilograms of food per day. They require a good amount of water also. They drink about one hundred and fifty to two hundred liters of water every day, in addition to the amount of water they use to pour over their bodies to cool themselves. Water is lost from the body mostly through urine and breath. Almost forty liters of water is lost daily as urine and excreta, and almost twenty liters are lost in breathing. They cannot extend their tongue outside, as seen in many other animals, and the trunk compensates for that deficiency to some extent.

Elephants enjoying water

Almost 90 percent of breathing is carried out through the trunk. Elephants cannot breathe properly through their mouths like many other animals. The activities done by the trunk are another unique peculiarity of elephants. A trunk has more than one hundred thousand of muscles which allow it to shorten, extend, and twist it as they wish. Usually, for any other animal to do these types of activities they need a bone to support or a fulcrum arrangement; however, elephants can move their trunks without any of these facilities.

The respiratory process in the elephant is also unique. Mammals in general take air inside (inspire) by creating a negative pressure in the chest cavity around lungs by mainly lowering the diaphragm. However, elephants can inspire by the use of special respiratory muscles. All land mammals have pleura in the thoracic cavity except elephants.

Another interesting feature in elephants is their ability to move the penis without the help of a hip bone. There are several muscles to do this. This ability helps the male during mating to locate the vagina of the female. The vagina is located far below compared to other quadrupeds. Unlike other land mammals, the testicles in male elephants are located inside the abdominal cavity. Hemoglobin found in the red blood cells in elephants has very close similarities to whale hemoglobin, which supports the contention that elephants might have evolved from the sea animals. They can sleep in a standing position, usually, for a short period of time just before sunrise. Although they can walk at a high speed, they are not capable of running or jumping. Their digestion is poor. By looking at the feces, it is clear that much of the food is not digested fully. Elephants communicate well with each other. They use sound waves at a range of five hertz and twenty-four hertz, which can travel several kilometers. This range of soundwave cannot be heard by humans. Elephants are not behind any other animal in their ability to smell. They can recognize people by smell. This may be the reason why elephants go after fruits with smell rather than their color. Their ability to recognize colors is weak. Proof of this concept is obvious in their preference to jackfruits, whose smell spreads for a long distance when fully ripe.

Elephants do not have sweat glands. They control the body temperature by fanning their ears and putting dirt on their body surface. They can bring water from pouches, which are located on either side of the back of the throat, through the trunk and spray it on their body surface. They do all these activities to maintain their body temperature. The wrinkles on their skin also play a role in maintaining their body temperature by increasing the surface area. The term pachyderm" is used to denote the thickened skin of elephants and rhinoceros. The elephant's trunk is formed by the union of upper lip and nose. The total number of chromosomes for an elephant is fifty-six.

The elephant's heart has some peculiarities too. Its pointed end is split and is called "double apex." The actual use of this is not clear to scientists. Another peculiar thing is that the elephant has a small sensor, which is the size of a ping pong ball, on the upper palate, known as the "vomeronasal apparatus." This sensor is an organ that facilitates the animal's experience of smell. This has a unique function for mating. When females produce a specific smell during estrus, the males can detect and identify the females.

There is no gall bladder in elephants. Unlike the other herbivorous animals, the nipples are located between the forelimbs, like human beings. Nipples have several pores and milk comes through them. There is no udder per se. Since this is an animal that spends most of the time standing upright, the prevalence of arthritis is very high in elephants. If they don't walk regularly, they are more vulnerable to podiatric problems. The total number of bones in the skeleton of an elephant is 282. It is estimated that the vertebrae count could be between fifty-six and seventy-one. Since the patellae in the hind limbs are located way low, elephants are able to kneel down very low compared to other quadrupeds. It is quite interesting to note that animals such as comparatively short-necked elephants and long-necked giraffes have only seven cervical vertebrae. The cholesterol in the blood of elephant is between twenty-six and sixty-eight and glucose level is between sixty and 116.

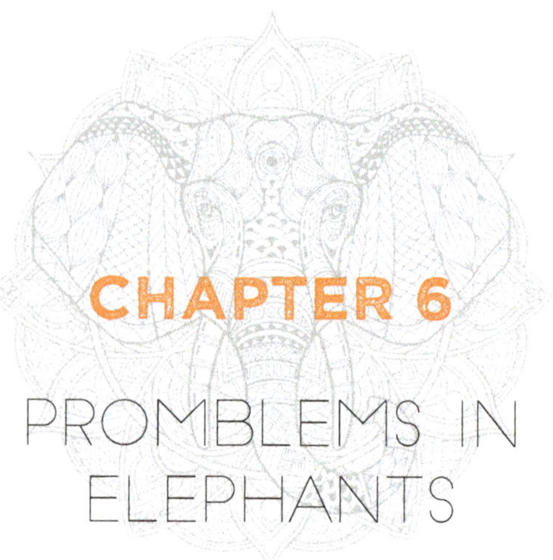

CHAPTER 6

PROMBLEMS IN ELEPHANTS

Drug addiction in elephants

This is the story of four elephants which became addicted to drugs. In recent years drug smuggling has become an important operation in Yunnan Province in Southern China, which borders with Myanmar (former Burma). Heroin smugglers use wild elephants to carry huge loads of heroin across the border in packages. When wild elephants roam and cross the border no one bothers them. In order to handle the wild elephants, they feed them fruits like banana laced with heroin. Heroin makes the animals docile and pliant. They get kind of sedated. When they cross the border with the package of drugs, the team members who are waiting on the other side feed them banana laced with heroin again to retrieve the load of narcotics they were carrying. Only the elephant handlers among the smugglers can approach them. This is frequently done with the same elephants. Eventually the elephants become addicted to narcotics. When they get addicted, they obey the orders of the handlers in anticipation of the rewards, drug-laced fruits. In addition, they show up regularly for the fruits at their doorsteps.

In this repeated process, the smugglers made these four wild elephants addicted to narcotics. Later, when they were caught by the police, the whole world came to know about these secretive, cruel, deceitful smugglers. When the officers knew what had happened to these elephants, they wanted to save them from the addiction. They called the elephants "Big Brothers." The rescuers never had any experience in treating addicted elephants. So, they decided to follow the same treatment program which physicians use for people. The elephants received extensive treatments in the drug rehabilitation center at a reserve in Yunnan Province. Each elephant was treated for more than a year with methadone along with other rehabilitation supportive treatments. Methadone is also a narcotic but has minimum adverse effects, such as addiction. When the elephants were brought to the rehabilitation center they were showing withdrawal symptoms and struggled so much that even heavy iron chains were broken. Methadone was given to the animals daily in gradually reducing doses over a course of a year until they did not need it anymore. The animals required five times the dose of methadone than human patients in the beginning to control the withdrawal symptoms. It was very difficult for the elephants to go through "cold turkey" symptoms, as it is for people. After one year of treatment, these animals were completely relieved from addiction. They did not have withdrawal symptoms and did not need methadone to control the symptoms.

The elephants are completely relieved from the addiction to heroin. Their health was satisfactory and they were released back to the forest to integrate into their herd to lead a natural life. The forest is now a protected area where many wild elephant live. The authorities suspect that there could be more drug addicted elephants in the wild. China declared that it is a crime to induce drug addiction in animals and those criminals are punishable by death. China is aggressively taking measures to capture such criminals.

Elephant, the drunkard

In Kerala State, India, it is not uncommon for elephants to be given illicit liquor by mahouts (elephant caretakers). Many of these mahouts are regular users of illicit liquor, so when they go to these shops, they offer the liquor to elephants as well. This type of behavior is seen in other states of India too.

An incident happened in December 1982 in a small place in India, near Bhutan. This north-eastern region of India borders with Bengal and Bhutan. It was in the evening and darkness was spreading throughout this north eastern region. One could vaguely see the movements of the villagers going home after purchasing groceries from the town. Dr. Cheeran and Mr. Summer Singh, then secretary of the ministry of Forest and Environment, were watching the villagers from a high point on the top of a hill. A cool breeze made it comfortable to enjoy the atmosphere, since the village is close to a river. Just like many other rivers in northern India, this river is also fairly wide but low in water level. Water flows only in the middle of the river. Because of the fog, the vision from one bank of the river to the other bank of the river is blurry. Dr. Cheeran and his friend could see something like a rock hill moving towards the middle of the river. Within a few moments, they figured out that it was an elephant herd. The villagers had previously tried several techniques, such as shots into the air, thunderbolt shots that make loud sounds, and tear gas shells to prevent the elephants coming to their village.

With this scene in the background, let us look into the history of the problem in the village. Dr. Cheeran had conversed with the minister of West Bengal about elephants attacking villagers and destroying their crops. The minister's opinion was that the villagers were hurting the animals. One villager had used a spear to hurt one of the elephants in the herd and the minister thought the elephants were coming back to attack the villagers to take revenge. Dr. Cheeran knew that this could not be the reason but did not tell the minister at the time. The next day the local newspaper reported that all the herds of elephant would be transported to anotherforest with the use of tranquillizers. The mission was impossible to implement because of the distance to the forest. From Calcutta (Kolkata) you have to travel more than one hour by plane to reach Bagdogra airport, which is the closest airport to the village. Because of the distance, the elephants would have to be airlifted. This was impossible and unimaginable. Dr. Cheeran talked to the higher authorities in the district and explained to them that the reason for the attack by elephant was not due to revenge and the actual cause had to be determined or the problem would remain unsolved.

Fortunately, Dr. Cheeran and the district collector and the superintendent of police hail from the same state in India. This helped the author to get the superintendent's attention and eventually convince him to make further inquiries, which gave more interesting insight into the reason for the elephant attacks. The villagers were experts in making illicit liquors. They make it in large quantities. Raw materials such as unrefined brown sugar and fruit juices are filled in large drums and then buried in the sand on the banks of the river, where there is no water, to allow fermentation. The fermented liquid is later distilled to make concentrated liquor. Elephants have great sniffing power, so they were able to identify the drums with fermented liquid by their smell. The fermented liquid had a sweet and sour taste which elephants like. The elephants routinely came to get the fermented liquid (brew) from the drums. The fact is that the good taste and the euphoric feeling after they drank made the elephants more attracted to this crude liquor and they were getting kind of addicted to this. They could not control their desire to drink it more and more, just like alcoholics in the society. In the beginning of this illicit business, the villagers buried the drums on the other side of the river close to the forest. But when the attacks came frequently, they gradually moved the business close to the village. A narrow stream of water separated the two sides. At that time, the village was a "dry" area (alcohol prohibition area), and the police interfered and they had to give up this side-business completely. However, the "dumb drunkards" (elephants) did not know this change and kept on searching for the crude liquor. Subsequently, they started to enter into the village. After entering they found grain storage in the village, in addition to bananas, coconut seedlings, and other leafy plants. In this process of their search for liquor, they began to demolish small huts in the village.

Around this is the time, Mr. Peace, an expert in electrifying fences to protect villagers from wild elephants, came to this area from Australia. A new problem came up at that time. Where to put the fence? If it was on the side of the village, the villagers couldn't get water. On the other hand, if it was on the other side of the river, the elephants couldn't get water. Finally, the fence was erected on the side of the village with a gate and a timed schedule for the villagers' use.

Another interesting incident happened in Palakkad district in Kerala State. A big tusker got upset and started behaving unusually. Nobody knew the reason for this behavior. So, Dr. Cheeran was called to tranquilize the elephant, assuming that the bad behavior was due to musth. When the author and his team reached there, they found that the elephant and the mahout were "regulars" at the toddy shop. That particular evening, since the "regulars" were late, the owner of the shop, without waiting for the "regulars," closed the shop and went home. The elephant got so angry that he got into the shop and drank the left-over toddy. He also drank the artificial toddy ingredients, which were kept in a solution for fermentation to be used the next day. Ironically, this type of artificial toddy is called locally "the elephant tranquilizer." As the name indicates, this toddy can give a person a "high kick." After drinking all these items, the tusker became really drunk. So the team, knowing all this information, did not want to use anymore tranquilizer on the elephant. They decided to wait till the sunrise. In order to prevent any problems with "live wire" (electric shock), the electric city board was called to turn off the main switch to the area. In the early morning, all was well and the elephant became obedient as usual when his "kick" was over.

Another incident of an elephant drinking solution kept for fermentation happened in the northeastern state of Assam. Villagers usually use rice flour in solution for fermentation. They also use crushed Mahowa flower (common in the forest during spring) for fermentation. The spring season is dangerous because villagers and elephants have confrontations over fermented liquor. A few years ago, wild elephants came to the village and drank the fermented liquor and got drunk. Six villagers were killed in that incident.

Some intoxicating fruits

There are several stories about African elephants' passion for liquor. Elephants have an intense attraction to marula, a fruit commonly found in South Africa. The marula tree is very similar to the mango tree found in different parts of the world. It reaches a height of ten to fifteen feet, and the top portion of the tree is spread like an umbrella. The color of the fruit is yellow and is used to make jam and also different varieties of liquors. Elephants have a craving for these fruits. People believe that the fruit gets fermented in the digestive system of elephants after eating and turns into liquor which gives a euphoric "kick" to the animal. However, Steve Morris, a scientist at Bristol University, disagrees. His argument is that if the animal weighs about 3.5 tons (a fairly small elephant compared to African elephants in general), it needs 1.8 liters of pure liquor to get drunk. That means that the elephant has to eat a lot of fruit. The fruit has only 7 percent alcohol in it, so this is impossible. This raises a question of why the animal has a craving for this fruit. The belief that elephants are getting drunk by eating this fruit prompted the people of South Africa to make an expensive liquor, Amarula, available commercially. Marula fruit juice, after fermentation and distillation, is kept in closed containers for almost two years for aging. Into this liquor they add the pulp of the fruit as a cream to increase the taste of the liquor. It is a common practice to give a bottle of this liquor as a gift to every foreign visitor at the Tembe Elephant Breeding Station, as a token of their appreciation.

Among other stories, there are instances where elephants can get intoxicated on substances other than toddy, fermented liquid, or Amarula. One such instance that happened in Russia is worth mentioning. On a very cold day, when the temperature was far below freezing (-30°C), a mahout got an idea. He thought the elephant might need vodka for "warming up" just like him. He gave a bucket full of vodka to the elephant. Within minutes the elephant started getting the "kick." He became very naughty initially and then became aggressive and violent and broke the heater and hot water pipe. During this violent activity, the elephant suffered some burns on his body, which made him even more violent. This vicious cycle lasted several hours before the elephant calmed down.

"Pink Elephant" is an expression used to describe the condition of a drunk. This can be explained by the following example. If you show one finger to a drunkard and ask him how many there are, he will say two. This stage is called "Pink Elephant."

A lazy bum elephant

Generally speaking, elephants are good workers. However, you might occasionally come across some "lazy bums" in some herds of elephants. Captive elephants are used mostly for parades, processions, and temple ceremonies. However, they are also used for work in the forest for timber logging. These captive elephants are hired by the contractors who have taken bids for timber logging. The elephants come from different owners because one owner may not be able to supply all required elephants. They are hired with their mahouts (caretakers) and the hired elephants are taken to the forest and are camped in the vicinity of the timber logging area. Timber logging is hard work, so in those camps different types of elephants can be seen. Some are good workers and occasionally some are lazy bums. The bums will show uncomfortable behavior as soon as they are taken to the timber piles. In fact, they express their unwillingness before the actual work even begins.

Many readers do not realize that such behavior exists among wild elephants. Dr. Cheeran had an occasion to note one such elephant during the operation of an elephant transfer from Dodpetta forest to Nagarhole Wildlife Sanctuary in the state of Karnataka, India. This wild elephant tried to fool the team of officials, making it a learning experience for everyone involved.

The transferring process involves several steps. First, the elephant has to be tranquilized. Then ropes are put on its four legs. Two rope ends of the hind legs are fastened to two big trees. These ropes are loosened as necessary when the animal moves forward. The other two rope ends are then fastened to one hind leg of each captive elephant. These two captive elephants are well trained for this purpose. Usually, captive elephants are large males and very obedient to the commands of the mahouts. The veterinary doctor's team will take care of the wounds, if any, on the wild elephant and then all nonessential members in the team will be asked to move away. Only then will the veterinarian give the antidote for the tranquilizer.

On the day of operation, the team starts very early in the morning, as usual, when the wild elephants are more often seen. Since the whole operation is performed in the forest, every team member has to pack and carry his own breakfast and lunch, which usually consists of eggs, fruits, and bread. When the first part of the operation is over (when tranquilization of elephant is achieved), everyone takes a break for breakfast. As planned on that day, the darter was able to tranquilize a fairly large tusker. Immediately, the team started putting ropes on all four legs of the wild animal. The ropes of the hind legs were tied to the trees and ropes of the front legs were tied to the hind leg of the captive elephant. Once the wild animal was secured like this, the antidote was given. The elephant was able to stand up and take a couple of steps forward. The ropes on the hind legs were loosened as needed. However, he did not want to continue forward.

There is a unique way an elephant shows his hesitation or unwillingness to move. He will put the front of his head on a tree, as if he is going to push the tree down and hesitates. He will not apply any force to the tree. Somehow, if you are successful in moving the elephant forward, he will do the same thing again with another tree after a few steps. There is no shortage of trees in the forest, so this is a frequent technique. Another technique the elephant uses is to kneel down to the ground and simulate crawling. Some animals do this not because they are lazy but because of their apprehension about the event.

In this particular case, the elephant that was tranquilized was a large one in size and height. When he stood up after the antidote, he walked a few steps forward then stopped at a tree, repeating this process a couple of times. Then, he started moving in the crawling fashion for some more time, then suddenly fell down sideways and did not get up. The mahouts tried all possible methods to get him up, but all in vain. The sun had risen and it started getting hot. Since it is not a good idea to wait for long time in the hot sun, the members of the team and the rest of group were frantically thinking of how to tackle the situation. Everyone started looking at each other. The forest officers had some doubts about the dose of tranquilizer and they suspected that when an animal was able to walk after tranquilization and suddenly dropped to the floor it may be due to overdose. But Dr. Cheeran was confident that the dose could not be too high, because the elephant responded after tranquilization without any unusual reactions. In addition, the elephant was above average in size and could easily tolerate a dose for the average elephant. All his vital signs were as expected at the time of tranquilization. So, there wasn't any reason to suspect overdose. Dr. Cheeran's concern was more about any fracture of bones during the fall when the tranquilizer was fired. At this point, it is worth mentioning that bones of elephants are less strong compared to other species of mammals. So, when they fall, due to their massive body weight, there is a likelihood of getting bone fractures, especially when the impact is sudden and hard.

The time was close to noon and everyone was tired and hungry. Many times, the team faces obstacles that are totally unexpected. They come quickly and without any indication—a kind of "Murphy's law." To solve the problem, Dr. Cheeran suggested a solution: Take the ropes from the captive elephants and tie the wild elephant to strong trees and then everyone leaves the premises, including the captive elephants, so that the wild elephant would be alone but would be unable to run away. He also suggested no one should go too far, but just vanish from the sight of the wild elephant. Since it was a thick forest with many trees, this was easily accomplished and they could have their breakfast. This plan was well received due to their eagerness to solve the problem and also because everyone was hungry. One fellow was assigned to watch the elephant by resting in a hideout. The entire group implemented the plan, started consuming their food, and gave some bushes and leaves to the captive elephants as food. Within a short period of time, and before they finished their breakfast, the watchman came running happily to inform the team that the elephant had already stood up. He also said that the elephant did not show any difficulty in standing up, which was very comforting to the forest officers, indicating it was not an overdose. It was even more comforting to Dr. Cheeran that it was not a case of broken bones. Everyone relaxed and noted this somewhat amusing experience had become a valuable lesson. It demonstrated not only the elephant's intelligence, but his skillful strategy to avoid work! Ultimately, he was relocated to his new home in the wildlife sanctuary in Karnataka, India.

Elephants becoming aggressive

Nowadays, common news in Kerala State is that elephants are getting more furious than usual and attacking mahouts and the public. They hurt mahouts and even kill them. People say that this is due to the cruelty of mahouts towards elephants. On the other hand, older generations mahouts say that it is the inexperience of the new generation mahouts causing this problem. If you take an impartial stand, both are correct to some extent. In order to analyze this matter, let us discuss the nature of behavior in elephants. This would be the best approach to get to the bottom of the problem and perhaps to a realistic conclusion. Elephants' behavior can be broadly classified into three categories. The first is obedience, the second is disobedience, and the third is attack. How do they get these behavioral manifestations? Let us analyze.

Elephant should obey: We all expect an elephant should be obedient. This expectation shows selfishness of people. Many times we forget how elephants came to be a "pet" animal. In reality, almost all elephants in Kerala are captured from the wild. That means they were all free-roaming animals in the forest. They were born and raised in the wild. We capture them by the using deceptive traps and then train them to obey commands. This training comprises cruelty too. When they are in a situation from which there is no escape, they start obeying. In other words, they tolerate mahouts because elephants have no other option. So, our expectation that an elephant should be obedient is a misconception. It is still a wild animal to a large extent.

Obedience: When the elephant starts obeying the commands, we consider them tamed. In order to tame an elephant, there are two important factors. The first one is the elephant's natural ability to obey commands. The second is its ability to understand the command (intelligence) and also to remember it (memory power). Wild animals like tigers and cheetahs cannot be tamed like elephants. What is the special factor in elephants? By nature, elephants live in groups called herds in the wild. Tigers and other wild animals are "loners" or "singleton" animals. They live alone. Elephants are different from those "loner" animals. It would be more appropriate to say that elephants live in large families. If they live together with different families, scientists call the group "clan." The head of the family is usually the oldest female elephant, not a tusker. Naturally, obedience, which is a must in a family life, is seen in elephants. That means elephants are born with the ability to live in a herd as we live in a society. Obedience is the most important asset in its life.

The next factor is the intelligence. Elephants are well-known for their intelligence. This has been proven recently by scientific experiments. The studies to determine the ratio of weight of brain and the body are part of these experiments. Memory is also associated with intelligence. The hippocampus is an area of the brain and it is the center for remembering commands (memory power). This is well-developed in elephants.

Let us go back to the topic of obedience in the elephant. Three reasons are responsible for obedience: fear, respect/trust, and love. The first duty of the trainer of a wild elephant is to infuse these emotions into the animal in moderate levels to control it. Creating a balance of these emotions in elephants is the primary factor that will make a good mahout. The most important emotional factors are love and trust, to keep the elephant under control. In the long run, the mahout will provide love and affection to elephants to get obedience in return. During the training of an elephant (taming), there will be some unpleasant experiences. There will be a tendency in any animal to react to an unpleasant experience by hurting the person causing it. Scientific investigations have confirmed this behavior in animals. As elephants are intelligent animals, they understand the concept of cause and effect.

Disobedience: There are two or more reasons for this. First is the pressure they experience mentally and bodily. For example, elephants undergo tremendous stress when they are subjected to back-to-back work in temple festivals without any rest, and in some cases without food, water, or proper sleep. There were occasions in temple compounds where elephants did not get proper food or drink and mahouts got "improper" drink (alcohol spiked drinks), and the elephants became wild and angry.

The second factor for disobedience is the lack of interaction between the mahout and the elephant. There should be a close and long interaction and association to create a bond between man and animal. Nowadays, the mahouts come and go. They don't get close to or engage in long interactions with their elephants. Sometime the analogy for this is like hiring a different driver for your own car every day. When you analyze the new reports of elephants becoming aggressive, you come to know that the mahouts were with the elephants only for a couple of weeks or so, not enough time to establish rapport.

In many cases, the mahout that was attacked by an elephant had only a couple of weeks' interaction with the elephant. His control over the elephant was very limited. Another cause is that when the primary mahout gets busy, he allows the second mahouts to handle the elephant in festivals. His commands may not be appreciated by the elephant. It is also a fact that when a person buys an elephant, he may not get an experienced mahout. The training needed to become a mahout is hard and risky. Many times they have only very limited practical experience with live elephants. It takes many years to make a good mahout. As you know, it is not possible to become a driver by reading driver's manual. So, a mahout has to work as an apprentice to a primary (chief) mahout for several years before becoming a primary mahout himself.

In addition to all these problems, in most of the festivals there will be a competition. Naturally when there is a competition, most likely there will be some foul play also. In such cases, they tend to hurt the elephant, which will aggravate the elephant more and he will respond with more aggression. The role of the organizers of the festival and locals to provoke elephants is not at all small. All their attention is concentrated on the success of the festival, not on the welfare of the elephants. Elephants don't get proper rest, food, or water on time. They have to stand on concrete or bituminized places in hot tropical summer for a long time. Most festivals that use elephants start at noon and extend to night.

Another factor is the fantasies of people. It is prestigious to show that your favorite elephant can keep its head way up. In order to do that, the mahouts poke the lower jaw area with sharp object. This area is highly sensitive and painful for the elephant. The elephant becomes more furious, to a "break point." Then the mahout loses control over the elephant. When this happens with the elephant and the mahouts, the people gathered there will get excited and do all kinds of "cheerleading" actions, which will make the scene go from bad to worse. They scream, sometime throw stones, show flame torches, and make noise, beating on tins. All this incites an elephant to run amok. The elephant may be either frightened or furious. When the elephant runs, these people follow in big crowds, shouting at the animal. The other elephants in the function will also start running, mainly because of apprehension. The ultimate result of this can be loss of people and other animals' lives, damage to the property, and total chaos of the entire area.

Musth and elephants' revenge

Musth in elephants is a familiar term for Keralites (people from Kerala State, India). Locally it is called *madham* and those who are associated with elephants call this condition *neere*. It is an uncontrolled emotional urge of healthy young- adult male elephants. It is not similar to rut, which is a behavior of deer during breeding season.

Musth is a condition seen in male adult elephants every year, more or less at the same time. *Madham Pottal*, a term used for this condition, literally means "crazy explosion." It does not occur in cow elephants. However,it was believed that it can occur in African cow elephants but later on, further investigations proved that it does not occur in females. In elephants, a gland associated with this condition (musth gland) is located between the ear and eyes. It has a slit opening from which a fluid oozes out during the time of musth. Signs of musth occur in elephants when they reach an age close to twenty.

Elephant in initial stage of musth

At that age, an elephant may not show a full-fledged sign of musth. Locally, this insignificant sign is called *moda*. During this time the animal does not obey to the commands of the mahout, the elephant caretaker. Sometimes the animal may even try to attack him.

After passing through more than couple of *modas* (four to five years later), the elephant begins to show signs of a fully developed musth. The musth gland swells up and the fluid, with a peculiar smell, starts flowing, little by little initially and later copiously. This confirms the beginning of musth. There are three stages for musth and altogether the musth period lasts for about one to three months. The initial stage of a three-month musth shows signs such as behavioral problems and disobeying commands, which lasts for about three weeks. The next stage is a full-fledged period characterized by violent and aggressive behavior, such as attacking other animals, people, and destruction of properties. This period lasts for a month. This is followed by a post-musth period that lasts for another month. This is a recovery period, but people still have to be careful with the animal.

Apart from these external signs, the testosterone level in the blood of the animal increases exponentially (ten to sixtyfold increase). Naturally, this increases the aggressiveness of the animal. The elephant will not obey the commands of the mahout and sometimes chases him. It will be ready to attack the mahout. Since the male hormone testosterone increases, its sexual desire or libido increases. It may be seen masturbating. The general belief is that these elephants in captivity are showing all this aggression because they cannot mate with female elephants. However, musth is also prevalent in the wildlife where males and females have free access. During the musth phase, even a small elephant will be willing to fight with a large tusker. Therefore, most of the time other elephants won't even dare to fight with an elephant in musth. If you are travelling in the forest on the back of a trained captive elephant, this elephant will raise its trunk to catch the smell of the wild elephants in musth and will hesitate to go in that direction. This shows that not only people but also other elephants try to avoid an elephant in musth.

Although sexual desire and activity in males increases during the musth time, they can also mate with females even when they are not in musth. They have the ability to reproduce during all seasons of the year, just like human beings. All other animals may not have this ability. For example, in dogs it is seasonal. When a male elephant urinates normally, its penis comes out. However, during musth time, urine dribbles drop by drop or leaks gradually from the penis. Sometimes, the color of the urine turns whitish. It used to be believed to be semen. However, when the urine was tested, scientists could not find any sperm in it.

During musth, if an elephant attacks a person at all, it's the chief mahout (the primary caretaker). When the trainer or the primary mahout gives punishment to the elephant we call it "teaching a lesson." But always remember elephants will be waiting for an opportunity to teach a lesson in return. In general, control or management of an elephant is carried out by establishing dominance over the elephant. During musth an elephant will try to break this dominance over him.

There are two reasons for an elephant attacking the chief mahout. During day-to-day management, there will be several punishments, however silly they might be, given by the chief mahout to the elephant. These punishments are given to make the elephant learn and remember some important commands. This is actually a process of establishing dominance over the elephant. However, the elephant does not take it that way and he stores those punishments in the back of his memory. He will not show any signs of his displeasure at the time of punishments and hides his revenge in the back of his mind. He continues to behave as if nothing has happened. When he gets a chance to take revenge, he will use it. Musth is the time for it. During musth he is totally different psychologically. He does not realize the change in behavior. According to elephant enthusiasts, the revenge he stored in his subconscious mind comes out uncontrolled.

As mentioned above, during musth the male hormone testosterone production is increased tremendously. This situation can be compared to a bullock (castrated male cattle) turning to a bull (uncastrated male cattle). In musth, the elephant's mindset to live in the society which includes accepting hierarchy (organization in the herd) is lost. It is more or less like our teenage children. In the elephant, it turns completely upside down. This condition is called "inverse dominance." The best way to handle this situation is to let the secondary mahout handle the elephant. In almost all cases of elephant attacks that have occurred in Kerala State, the primary mahout was the target. The elephant does not have any revenge towards the secondary mahout because he seldom gives dominating commands or punishments on a daily basis. So, no revenge is stored in the elephant's subconscious mind against the secondary mahout. Usually, the primary mahout does not hand over the control immediately, mainly because of his ego, and in some cases the economic factors. When the secondary mahout takes over the job, the mahout loses the "important status" and in some cases may have a cut in pay. So he will postpone as much as possible in assigning the job to the secondary mahout, thinking that the condition of the elephant will improve in the near future. This attitude leads to disaster. Sometimes, the owner of the elephant interferes and makes things straight. If not, one fine morning the elephant reaches his "break-point" by surprise. The elephant breaks all rules and hierarchal barriers and also all physical barriers and runs amok. In this process he can cause death and damage to properties. This leads to chaos all around. Finally, it ends up with tranquilizer shots and chaining of elephants.

In the wild, during musth a young adult male will challenge the hierarchy of the old male in the herd, whom he considers his rival. Again, the analogy will be teenagers questioning parents.

You can say testosterone is the culprit but it is not necessarily related to sexual behavior. In olden days in the Kerala State, when timber-logging male elephants were in musth, mahouts allowed them to go to the forest so that they could mate with female elephants in the wild. The female estrus cycle lasts for about three weeks. This is a receptive time for cow elephants. Conception period is only three to five days. During this time, they copulate many times. Males stay with the females for a few more days after copulation. Even with this, when the male in musth returns from the forest he will still show aggressive behavior, suggesting that sexual satisfaction does not solve the problem of musth.

Although it is believed to be the revenge of the animal towards the chief mahout for all the punishment he has given to the animal previously, this assumption is not completely true. It is a behavioral problem of the animal against the hierarchy. Young adult elephants question or challenge the existing hierarchy or authority, either within the herd or between animal and man. They want to disobey the rules and existing dominance imposed on them by the social environment. Under normal conditions, being social animals, elephants accept the organizational dominance. However, during musth their mental attitude changes to these rules. Their aggressiveness reaches a peak and they are willing to face any danger or adverse environment. They become daredevils. For this reason, when other elephants see an elephant in musth they try to avoid them. Elephants in musth do not want to accept dominance by other elephants or by humans.

The interesting phenomenon is that those who usually manage to get things done with the elephant with love can still do it when the animal is in musth. An incident that occurred in Thrissur, Kerala State, is worth mentioning here. One of the largest elephants in Thrissur was in musth and everyone was afraid of approaching him. However, one old lady who used to feed him fruits was able to handle the elephant without much difficulty. She asked him to do different maneuvers by giving commands such as sit down, come close, and go back, without any problem. The elephant always obeyed her, even during the musth time. This is because the old lady never dominated him. All she did was that she loved him dearly.

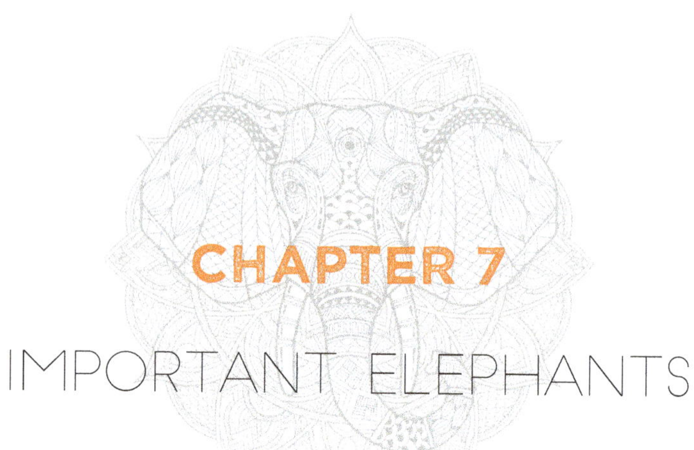

CHAPTER 7

IMPORTANT ELEPHANTS

An unusual elephant

Some Hindu mythological books and some local medical textbooks give suggestions about wings on elephants. The story goes like this: Once an elephant was flying over a holy place where *maharishis* (Holy men) were performing *poojas* (holy rituals) and it defecated and the dung fell on the *pooja* spot. The chief *maharishi* got so angry and cursed the elephant. Thus, the elephant lost its wings and lost his ability to fly. The *maharishi's* angry response was understandable. Just imagine the feeling one has when a bird defecates on the clothes of a person going to a wedding reception. There is a painting of a flying elephant in the famous Saraswathi Mahal library in Thanjavoor, Tamil Nadu State, India. Flying ability of elephants is also mentioned in *Hasti-vidyarnava*, one of the oldest and most famous books in the Assamese language. One thing is for sure: The largest plane in the world, Boing 747, is named "jumbo jet" after the largest elephant in the world, Jumbo. The jet was introduced in 1970 and has a capacity to carry four hundred to 524 passengers. It is seventy-one meters long, has a sixty-meter wing span, and can fly carrying four hundred tons. It is a flying castle. No wonder such a plane got the name of the largest captive elephant that once lived on earth.

Now the question pops up, who was Jumbo the elephant? The short answer is that he was the world's most famous elephant. There is an interesting history about this African elephant. He was a resident of the London Zoo between 1865 and 1882. He was number one in size in Europe, perhaps in the world. The term "jumbo" captured the attention of everybody and always meant "something very big" after this elephant.

Let us look into some of the facts about Jumbo the elephant. Somewhere around 1861, he was captured at a young age from Abyssinia in Ethiopia and was sold by Arabian merchants to an individual in Cairo, Egypt. From there he was sold to a zoo in Paris, France. Later, the authorities in the Paris Zoo gave him to the London Zoo in exchange for a rhinoceros or hippopotamus. Thus, Jumbo arrived in the London Zoo on June 26, 1865. He was only 122 centimeters (four feet) tall, and was an unattractive baby elephant. The word "jumbo" was not in the English language at that time. It is believed that the name came from a word in an African language that meant "elephant." Another version is that the name Jumbo came from Swahili, an African language. In this language, "jumbo" means "leader" or "head" of the group. Whatever the origin of the name, Jumbo, during his twenty-five years of life, reached the pinnacle of his fame all over the world. Mr. Abraham Bartlett, then administrator of the London Zoo, appointed Mr. Matthew Scott as the caretaker and trainer of Jumbo. Jumbo was very lean, thin, and unimpressive in appearance at that time.

The first sign of musth in elephants is called moda. At that time the elephants won't show the typical signs and behavioral changes of a full-fledged musth. A couple of years after his arrival in London Zoo, Jumbo started showing signs of moda. At that time, he allowed only Mr. Scott to come close to him. In later years, he showed typical signs of musth. At that time, he did not even allow Scott to come close to him. This incidence of musth and subsequent behavioral changes in the elephant were all new to the western zoo officials. They allowed Jumbo to let loose and go outside his pen to reduce his intense behavioral problems. Although it produced a temporary improvement in his behavior, it did not abate the intensity of problems. Later on, his problems due to musth became so intense that he became violent. This forced the caretakers to put him in a cage, which made him more aggressive. He tried to get out of the cage and used his tusks to pry open the cage bars. In that process, he broke both tusks. The tusks began to grow under his eyes, instead of below the ears. This unusual growth got infected and inflamed. The pain was intense and he became more violent. They tried to starve him to reduce his aggressiveness, just like many caretakers did locally, particularly in some parts of Kerala State, India. Jumbo became very weak and did not lie down. It is believed that when elephants are weak and very tired, they won't lie down, thinking that they may not be able to get up. So, Jumbo slept in a standing position leaning to the cage bars. Weeks passed by. He became more violent, frustrated, and dejected. The infected teeth (growing tusks) got worse and swelled up with intense pain. Mr. Bartlett and Mr. Scott got an adventurous idea to stop the pain. They decided to cut open his infected and inflamed boil. They made a long stick, forty-five centimeters long, with a sharp and pointed curvy blade at the tip. The stick looked more or less like the stick that is used by mahouts in Kerala.

Bartlett and Scott prepared for their adventurous activity by asking all workers to get out of the cage. They both decided to go into the cage. They knew that anything could happen to them. They came close to the body of the animal and stood touching the elephant at the sides, the safest place to stand while handling the elephant. They slowly lifted the stick with the sharp blade to cut open the boil. At that time, to their surprise and everyone's surprise outside the cage, Jumbo himself pointed out the exact place of the boil where it was hurting him! Without wasting even a second or thinking twice, they put the hook into the boil and pulled it down. A lot of pus and blood gushed out. Immediately, the elephant screamed and moved away from them but did not attack or hurt them. Then he came close to them as if he was thanking them for their help. This behavior of the elephant gave them confidence to clean the boil with a syringe and drain the pus completely.

With this procedure, they took care of the problem on one side, but what about the other side? If they did not do the other side, the work was not complete. While the caretakers were thinking about it, Jumbo turned to the other side and showed them the problem. They were able to do the same surgical method on the other side with the cooperation of Jumbo. The whole adventurous activity they carried out may not be a big deal now with modern facilities, but back then, with the limited knowledge of elephants' behavior and cooperation, it was indeed a marvelous surgical procedure. For them it was a learning experience too. This incident gave them, and the western world, a large body of information about an elephant's understanding, love, and trust towards its mahouts and close associates. This incident was beautifully described by Mr. Bartlett in his book *Wild Animals in Captivity*, which was published after his death in 1898.

Jumbo safaris

After the healing of Jumbo's surgical wounds and subsiding signs of musth, the zoo official came up with a new idea. They decided to use Jumbo for safari, for those who visited the zoo. Trainer Scott had a vested interest in this new proposal. He thought that if this plan worked well, the zoo would get an estimated income of £200 and Mr. Scott would get handsome tips for giving elephant rides. The other trainers were jealous and turned their backs to this idea. This would create some problems in their life later on.

Eventually, Jumbo grew big and became a good pet elephant till the age of sixteen. However, this "good boy" status of Jumbo was interrupted on several occasions by his naughty behavior. This naughty behavior troubled the zoo authorities tremendously. As a precaution, they bought a shot gun to use as a last resort in case something terrible happened. In those days there were no tranquillizers to control the elephant in musth when they ran amok. They even thought about getting rid of him; however, they continued to use Jumbo because their customers were world famous people. To mention a few, the riding dignitaries were Her Highness Queen Elizabeth, American President Theodore Roosevelt, British Prime Minister Winston Churchill, and Barnum Circus owner, Mr. Barnum. By that time, Jumbo's fame crossed the Atlantic and reached America. Mr. Barnum, a wealthy man, had his eye on Jumbo. He also understood the dilemma of the London Zoo officials and he knew if he made a good offer to purchase Jumbo, they would not reject it. He came up with an offer of £2,000 and they accepted.

When Mr. Barnum put forth the deal to London Zoo officials, they had a pleasant surprise. Although Jumbo was behaving fine without much problem, the London Zoo officials were looking for an opportunity to get rid of Jumbo. They thought it was a blessing in disguise. So, the deal went through without any hesitation. According to the contract, the transportation of the elephant and its expenses were the responsibility of Mr. Barnum, to which he agreed. When the news of the deal was leaked, the *Times* newspaper reported with a catchy headline that "Briton is selling its prestige." This was reported in January 25, 1882. Most of the "British think tanks" were stunned and upset with this deal; however, Mr. Barnum, who knew the consequences of media publicity, toned down the bad publicity. He said in a press conference that giving Jumbo was a friendly gesture on Britain's part and helped the understanding between the two countries, and that Jumbo would be a British ambassador to America and its people. The rumor is that even the Queen tried to persuade Barnum to back off from the deal. However, Barnum strongly stood on his word and responded that "the deal is a deal."

Five to six weeks later, the agent of Mr. Barnum arrived at London Zoo with a mahout. They also brought a cage for Jumbo that was made of oak wood and reinforced with iron belts all around it. They asked Mr. Scott, who was the trainer of Jumbo, to instruct Jumbo to get into the cage. This is when Scott tried some foul play. He complained that for whatever reason, Jumbo was not getting into the cage. This news reached Barnum in America, who used this news for publicity about Jumbo. All over America, everyone knew that Jumbo was coming to America. Mr. Bartlett understood the real reason why Jumbo refused to get into his cage. So he had a secret discussion with Scott and gave him a lucrative offer, along with some threats. The offer was that Scott would get £1,000 for letting the elephant into the cage and also would get a job in Barnum Circus with a good salary. Just in case he did not like the job in Barnum Circus, he would be given an alternative job in London. If he was not willing to do any of these, the new trainer, Newman, who came with the agent, would take over and Scott would lose his position. Mr. Bartlett abruptly stopped the conversation and walked away after giving him one day to think about it. Although the threat was intimidating, the offer was too good to refuse and Scott agreed to the deal. The very next morning, Jumbo was already in the cage. The reason for Scott's unusual behavior was he assumed he would lose his job if Jumbo was sold. Some elephant lovers might recall such an incident that happened in Kerala State, India. One mahout poisoned the elephant when he heard that the elephant was going to be sold. This type of foul play happens in every country in the world without exception.

Jumbo's walk to the ship was a heart-breaking event to all in London. The people gave a tearful and emotional send off to Jumbo, their favorite safari elephant. Regardless of their age and gender, people of London gathered on both sides of the road where Jumbo walked towards the ship. For the officials in the London Zoo, it was a big relief. Scott also decided to go to America with Jumbo. The cage with the elephant weighed more than thirteen tons and it was not an easy job to take Jumbo with the cage in a ship. The fare alone for Jumbo was more than $1,000 and the ship had to remove some of the other merchandise to accommodate Jumbo and the cage. In addition, they had to deny transportation of two hundred immigrant passengers who were planning to go to America on that ship.

At the port, the local citizens arranged a send-off party for Jumbo. Many dignitaries of London community attended the party and all wished him the best of luck and gave blessings to Jumbo for his trip and a wonderful future in America.

Jumbo, the American citizen

Mr. Barnum decided to make Jumbo's arrival a magnificent one. He distributed many pamphlets for publicity and finally on April 9, 1882, "the king of Assyria arrived." The brochure described Jumbo as "the sky-scraping King," "the wonder of the world," "the wonder the world has not seen before or will never see in the future." He also challenged that if anybody could show an elephant taller than Jumbo either in captivity or in the wild, that person will get one hundred thousand dollars. The publicity of Jumbo went overboard. They also made big beer mugs in Jumbo's name. There were sixteen horses in front to pull his cage and one elewphant to push. In that procession, Jumbo caught hold of the tail of a horse in front and did some naughty things. Mr. Barnum made every effort to make this procession of the colossal 11.5-foot-tall Jumbo a memorable event.

Mr. Barnum spent about thirty thousand dollars for the arrival of Jumbo. He showed Jumbo in exhibits and made $3,000 per day. Thus, within ten days, he was able to get back all the money he spent on Jumbo. Unfortunately, these golden days did not continue for very long. On September 15, 1885 Jumbo was taking part in a circus at St. Thomas, Ontario, Canada. Jumbo's job was to accompany each elephant that was introduced into the circus arena. A railway track line man who was in the audience enjoying the show forgot to close the track line. The train came so fast. The "cowcatcher" of the train caught a small elephant "Tom Thump" and pushed him away. Next was Jumbo. The train hit him severely. Jumbo did not die instantly. He was conscious but in a lot of pain. Mr. Scott screamed and wailed over Jumbo's body but soon Jumbo breathed his last. Although an exaggeration, it is said that to pull Jumbo's body from the railway track, they needed 160 horses.

Mr. Barnum was heart-broken and he brought a world-famous taxidermist, Mr. Henry Ward, from Rochester city to fix the body of Jumbo. He carried out the job very elegantly and Jumbo looked beautiful in his life size figure. It is said that during the post mortem of Jumbo, they were able to recover coins, medals, and bead chains from his stomach. In all communications, Mr. Barnum claimed that Jumbo was 11.5 feet (3.5 meters) tall, but according to Mr. Ward, Jumbo was only 10.95 feet tall (3.3 meters).

Mr. Barnum decided to ascend Jumbo to immortality. He gave the body of Jumbo to Tufts College in Boston. There, Jumbo also became the king. When examinations come close, students would go and put coins in his trunk as an offering, expecting good luck in their tests. Jumbo's skeleton itself weighed two tons. His full skeleton was donated to the Museum. In later years, during a fire, Jumbo's stuffed body was burnt to ashes. Although Mr. Barnum was depressed by this, he kept his spirit. He collected the ashes of Jumbo and placed them in an urn. The people of Boston considered Jumbo a lucky star. Mr. Barnum did not get frustrated and continued looking for an opportunity. He went to the London Zoo and purchased Jumbo's female companion elephant "Ales" and brought her to America. He tried to exhibit her as the "widow of Jumbo" but did not get much publicity and he failed in that venture.

Grandma Dakshayani

The oldest elephant in the world currently living is a captive elephant named Dakshayani. She is in a camp which is administered by the Travancore Devaswam Board, Kerala State, India. The board controls and maintains around 1250 temples in Southern Kerala, including the famous Sabarimala temple. Recently, they honored her with the title Grandma Dakshayani. According to the record of the Forest Department of Kerala State, she was eighty-seven years old in August 2018. Now she is qualified to get into the *Guinness World Records*.

The previous record in this category was held by a male elephant from Ling Wong, Taipei, Taiwan. This elephant died in February 26, 2003 at the age of eighty-six. Dakshayani is the first female elephant to get this recognition. She was owned by the king of Travancore, Kerala State. She was captured from Konni elephant forest at the age of five. Later, the king donated her to the Tiruvarat Kave temple, Attingal, Kerala State. From Tiruvarat Kave temple she was transferred to Chengalore Mahadeva Temple. She also holds a title for taking part in the maximum number of temple ceremonies. For more than fifty years she carried the idol of the Goddess of Sankmukam as a primary leading elephant in the temple festival. Physically, she is in good health except for a slight vision problem. She is a well-behaved captive elephant. During her entire life, there has not been a single incidence where she caused problems to anyone. According to her chief mahout, she becomes a little naughty sometimes, which her mahouts consider is a feather in her cap. Now she is not being used for the temple festivals except for very important functions. Two of her mahouts have already retired and she is enjoying her retired relaxing life.

She was honored at a big function that was inaugurated by Mr. Kadakampally, the minister in charge of Devaswam and Electricity Department of Kerala State. The function took place in Nandankode Sumangaly auditorium in Tiruvanandapuram, capital of Kerala State. The president of the Devaswam Board, Mr. Prayar Gopalakrishnan, was the chief guest of the function. In that function, Advocate K. Raju, the minister for Wildlife Department, honored Dakshayani with the title Grandma of Elephants.

Guruvayur Keshavan

Guruvayur Keshavan

Guruvayur is a municipal town in Thrissur district of Kerala State, India. The primary importance of the town is the famous Guruvayur Shri Krishna temple. There, the lord Shri Krishna is called "Guruvayurappan." Guruvayur Keshavan was a male elephant of the temple. The temple once had more than sixty elephants. Keshavan was the most famous elephant in the entire state of Kerala. He has been honored with many awards and titles of which the most important one is the title "Gajarajan" which means "king of elephants."These awards were given to him because of his majestic appearance, gentleness, intelligence, and extremely good conduct. In the later years of his life, he became a celebrity. He was captured from the Nilambur forest at a young age. The Nilambur royal family donated him to the Guruvayur Sri Krishna temple on January 4, 1922. Soon after his arrival, he became the favorite of the devotees of the temple and the local people. In the temple, he served the Lord Sri Krishna for about fifty-four years till his death. He was chosen unanimously to carry the idol of the deity during ceremonial functions of the temple. During his entire life, he never caused any bodily harm to anyone. He was noble in his character and kingly in his behavior.

He was 3.4 meters tall and majestic in his appearance. His life story was the theme of a movie in Malayalam language. The movie was entitled with his name and was released after his death. He died on December 2, 1976 at the age of seventy-two. He died on Guruvayur Ekadashi day, which is the most auspicious event of the temple. He served the lord even on the previous day of his death. When he was taking part in the temple function, he suddenly felt sick and the temple authorities removed the idol of the lord he was carrying. A team of veterinary doctors took care of him immediately. His day, however, had already arrived and the very next day he died. When devotees came to know that he was sick, they all gathered around him to pray for his life. The usual offering of devotees on Ekadashi day is fasting. Keshavan also fasted for the entire day, but a few minutes before his death, he stood up, took water in his trunk, and poured it three times on his body while all the devotees were watching him. Then he turned his head towards the deity, saluted the lord three times, and prostrated, keeping his trunk stretched and slightly raised, and died. All his actions were divine in nature, even at the time of his death. Many devotees cried hearing of his death.

A Tribute to late Guruvayur Keshavan

As a tribute to his services, the temple authorities erected a life-size statue of him. The anniversary of his death is still celebrated in Guruvayur. Several elephants of the temple take part in it. They arrive in a procession to his statue and put garlands on his head. They salute him one by one before they leave. Many dignitaries of the state take part in the ceremony. There are many stories about his intelligence, gentleness, and greatness. Some of stories include that he, even in the absence of his mahout, allowed the students to go first by yielding to them, cared for old and disabled people, and helped the authorities catch a thief red-handed in the temple premises. He would allow only those who hold the deity's idol to climb upon him, bending his front right leg and lifting it so that the person could hop onto him. All others had to climb up using his hind limbs.

Pitiable elephants as guinea pigs

A few years ago, an elephant by the name of Motola was brought for treatment to an elephant treatment center in Lampung, Thailand. The bottom of her foot was completely crushed and infected after she stepped on a land mine. Cambodia, the neighboring country of Thailand, had widespread use of land mines because of the previous skirmish involving Viet Cong fighters. Many places had warnings for people written in English and local languages, such as "don't walk here," "land mines are here," etc. to avoid accidents. Motola the elephant did not go to Cambodia willingly—she was taken there illegally by loggers to carry big logs of wood from the forest to the riverbanks. Since cutting trees in the forests of Thailand is prohibited by the government, almost two thousand elephants did not have any work assignments. However, in the border areas between Thailand and Myanmar (Burma), trees are cut illegally. This is the area where intense guerrilla warfare was carried out and land mines were a common military strategy used by these fighters. People who work there in the forest know about this situation and try to avoid it. They take amphetamine, a central nervous system stimulant and mind-altering drug, to deal with this drastic life-threatening situation. They give this drug to working elephants also. Both people and elephants work hard after taking this stimulant drug. The drug is available in plenty all over Cambodia. Thus, both mahouts and the elephants get addicted to amphetamine.

Another drug in this category is called "acid" in the secret code language in the underworld. This is actually Lysergic acid diethylamide (LSD). Dr. Cheeran heard more stories about this drug when he arrived in Oklahoma State in the United States. One of the bizarre stories is about the weird experiments of a scientist. In 1962, Dr. Louis Jolyon West, a psychiatrist cum scientist, tried to induce musth in Tusco, a tusker, by injecting 270 milligrams of LSD using a "capture gun." The tusker was little over three tons in weight. Instead of showing the signs of musth, the elephant started showing symptoms of epilepsy. Twenty minutes later, he gave 2.8 grams of Promazine, a tranquilizer, as an antidote. However, one hour and forty minutes after the first LSD dose, the elephant died and the cause of death of the elephant is still under debate among the scientists. They don't know which drug actually killed the elephant. The dose of LSD was thirty times higher than the dose allowed for elephants. The brain of an elephant is about three times of the weight of a human brain and the brain surface area (in African elephant) is about two and a half times greater than that of a human brain. The dose of Promazine given as an antidote was also high. Later, Dr. West admitted that the dose determined on the basis of body weight of the elephant was a mistake in this case. Dr. Ronal Siegel of UCLA conducted a similar experiment on two elephants. He used the same dose of LSD on body weight basis. He mixed LSD in water and gave it orally instead of injection. In that case, both elephants showed strange behavior but were not affected seriously and did not die.

Is he the most unfortunate elephant?

This is the story of an unlucky elephant. He is a captive elephant and is an inhabitant of the Prathapgund district in Utter Pradesh, India. His name is Mohan and he is about fifty-five years of age. Until recently he was used for many odd jobs, including begging for money, but now he is too weak even to beg.

Mohan was owned by the temple authority. Forest Wildlife officials of the state, local police, and the animal rights organization wanted to release him from the temple administration. The animal rights people, along with the

Wildlife officials, went to court and finally the court ordered him to be released to the forest wildlife authorities. However, the temple owners and the temple board would not release him. Finally, all the well-wishers of the elephant organized a protest for his release. The temple authorities kept the elephant in front of the temple and the elephant would bless the devotees by placing the tip of his trunk on the head of the devotees. After getting the blessing, the devotees would donate some money to the temple. Devotees gave whatever amount they could afford to give. In addition to this work, Mohan had to walk through the streets of the villages to collect money by offering blessings at least three times a week. This continued even after he was not able to walk. The temple authorities never provided any treatment for the elephant and if he did not walk, they forced him by inducing pain with pointed spears. When the wildlife authorities approached to determine the condition of the elephant based on the complaints from the animal rights organization, the elephant had some open wounds caused by the mahouts. This prompted the various animal rights organization to get involved in the release of the animal to the wildlife authorities. The court case lasted for several months. Finally, the district court got involved and came to a final decision in favor of the release. Along with Mohan, another elephant named Raju was in the same situation and was also released. Raju's health condition was also not satisfactory. He had been purchased by temple authorities ten years previously from Odisha, a neighboring state of Utter Pradesh. After getting the custody of elephants, the Utter Pradesh wildlife authorities said their primary objective was to take all the measures to recover the health of the two elephants.

The largest elephant in Zimbabwe killed

The largest elephant in Zimbabwe was killed by hunters from Germany. The hunters paid more than $50,000 as the fee for a hunting permit. This event happened in the Gonarezhou National Park in the south east region of Zimbabwe on October 8, 2015.

According to Zimbabwe's conservation task force, this elephant was the oldest and largest one in the entire country and probably in all of Africa. The park officials said that his tusks were so long that when he walked they almost touched the ground. Each of the unusually big tusks weighed fifty-five kilograms. After the hunting and killing of the elephant, the hunters took photos with the tusks. An experienced hunter acted as the hunters' guide and the photos were circulated on the social media. Many elephant enthusiasts gathered to raise their concerns, which forced them to remove the photos from social media.

The members of the hunting trip from Germany paid an enormous fee for a twenty-one-day hunting permit. The dead elephant was in his mid-forties. One report indicated that this elephant was not an inhabitant of the national park. They guessed that the elephant came from Kruger National Park and probably was killed when he was on his way to the Gonarezhou Park; however, some people disagree with this report. It is disappointing to many people that a local person who kills an elephant for food gets five-fifteen years of imprisonment, whereas a wealthy foreigner kills an elephant and walks away without any problem. In this case, he did it legally, paying a fee.

Not long ago, there was another incident of trophy hunting in Zimbabwe. The hunter, an American dentist, killed a lion named Cecil that was friendly with visitors. Although he was in the protected area from the visitors, he used to come out of his hideout area to greet the visitors. This he did for many years and it was a routine schedule for him, which is how the lion became friends with visitors. Killing that lion was a shock for the national park visitors. That incident also raised a lot of anger among the animal rights people against hunters. In this case, the hunter also had permission and a license to shoot and kill the animal.

Thus, in these cases both hunters were legal and neither hunter was prosecuted.

The white elephant

White elephant is a term that is commonly used appropriately and inappropriately in our daily conversations. Everyone knows the double meaning of this term. The Buddhist country Thailand is called land of white elephants. However, the concept and understanding of the term white elephant originated in India.

The famous mythic story of the churning of the "Ocean of Milk" is described in detail in Hindu mythology. During the churning, many items came out of the ocean. One of the products that came from ocean was a white elephant by the name of Iravatham, which was later given as a gift to Devendra, the lord of heavens who used it as his favorite vehicle to travel around the kingdom of heaven. The story is depicted in a famous sixteenth century painting in India at the time of the Mogul Dynasty. This painting is on exhibit at the Delhi museum.

There are several stories about white elephants in the Buddhist religion. Some Buddhists believe that even Siddhartha's (Buddha's original name) birth was due to a heavenly touch of a white elephant. His mother, Queen Mayadevi (wife of King Sudhodana), was blessed by a divine white elephant, which came from heaven. There are several such mentions about white elephants in this religion.

The white elephants mentioned in the Buddhist religion are not pure white. They look like elephants that did not have a bath for long time or those that are playing in the mud. Overall, they look more like light brown or greyish elephants. There are several criteria to consider an elephant as a white elephant in this religion. Once an elephant is considered white, then people have to take care of it with divine consideration. This divinity makes the elephant respected, sacred, and blessed. The chain to fasten the elephant cannot be made up of iron and is instead made of expensive metal, often gold or at least gold-plated. Their food bowls must also be gold-plated. Ordinary people cannot afford to keep them. Thus, a white elephant can be maintained only by kings and emperors.

Now let us look at the origin of this terminology. In olden days, kings in Siam (Thailand) used to give a white elephant as a present to a person in his cabinet (Lord or Duke) whom he did not like. Since these elephants have no utility value and are expensive to maintain, the gift soon made the duke or lord a pauper. This is the principle behind the term "white elephant." In this context, white elephant means anything that has no utility value and that is very difficult to maintain or is useless.

Moti, a very rare baby elephant

Dr. Cheeran was asked by several people during his tour to various countries whether it is possible for an African elephant to have a progeny with an Indian Elephant. Biologically the answer would be a big "no," because they belong to two different species.

However, the reality is different. Geographically, the mating of these two species in nature is difficult because they are found on two different continents, so mating is unlikely to happen. However, in zoos mating is possible because both African and Indian elephants coexist. This is what happened in the Chester Zoo in England. The Indian female elephant, Sheba, and the African male elephant, Jumbo Lino, mated and produced a baby elephant. This happened in 1978.

This crossbred baby elephant was named Moti. Unfortunately, Moti lived only ten days. Moti was evaluated and determined to be a crossbreed both phenotypically (by appearance) and genetically. There were some peculiar external features for Moti. The external features of both African and Indian elephants were seen in Moti. Moti had large ear lobes with pointed bottoms, similar to African elephants. The trunk had several folds, just like African elephants. However, at the end of the trunk, there was only one "finger," like the Indian elephants. African elephants have two fingers at the end of the trunk. Although the body looked like an African elephant, the top of the back did not have a depression. The back was slightly curved upward and looked more or less like the back of an Indian elephant.

The legs were slender and longer, like African elephants. However, each front leg had five nails and each rear leg had four nails, similar to the Indian elephants. The rare specimen of Moti is stuffed and kept for exhibition in a London museum.

Jap, the mother of elephant research

Although elephants are seen only in Africa and Asia, most of the elephant research is carried out in the Western world (Europe and America).

An elephant by the name of Japolina, with a nickname "Jap," lived in the twentieth century and was the first elephant that paved the path for elephant research. Francis G. Benedict was the director of Nutrition in Karin Institute, Washington, USA, who initiated the first elephant research. He compiled all the results of his experiments using Jap and published them as a book. This may be considered the first book on elephant studies and is still considered a reference book in elephant science.

Dr. Benedict had a passion to do metabolic studies in elephants. It took twenty-five years to fulfil his passion and he used Jap, a female elephant, for these research studies. Mr. P. T. Barnum, the owner of the well-known Barnum Circus, imported Jap from Europe in 1902. At that time, Jap was almost three years old. From 1920 to 1948, she was owned by several circus companies. Dr. Benedict saw her when she was with Gorman Circus Company in New Jersey. He was quite impressed by the good nature and friendliness of Jap.

At the first sight, Dr. Benedict decided that Jap would be the best elephant to study the physiology of elephants. His monumental study took almost fifteen months to complete. Based on this study, Dr. Benedict published a book consisting of two hundred pages. The title of the book is *Physiology of Elephants*. The findings of his research were consistent with the results of another study conducted later in sixty-four captive elephants. Thus, Dr. Benedict's book became the first reference book for physiological data on elephants.

Operation Ikki: Anatomy of elephants

It is true that a few years ago, scientists' knowledge about the "anatomy of elephants" was practically nothing. Dr. D. Mariappa, a well-known former anatomy professor and Dean of Madras Veterinary College, India, did some studies with an elephant fetus. This was the only information available at that time to the scientific world. It is interesting to note that the book form of his study on the elephant fetus was published by an American publisher. This book is out of print and is not available now.

On July 8, 1980, a female elephant by name Ikki died when a group of scientists were eagerly waiting for an opportunity to perform an elaborate study by dissecting an elephant carcass. Ikki was born in 1934 in Sri Lanka (former Ceylon). She was taken to Germany when she was two years old. Later, at the age of ten, she was taken to America. She died when she was in Florida, a south eastern state of the US. At the time of her death, she was owned by a circus company. Her dead body was taken to Detroit, Michigan, a state which is about 1500 kilometers away. There, her body underwent a detailed dissection study. Several tissue samples from various organs were taken for further histologic studies. Some samples were preserved for future studies. The entire study was organized by several groups of scientists interested in elephant research. The study resulted in obtaining several pieces of important information. One of the most surprising bits of information gained in that study was that an elephant trunk is made up of more than 150,000 muscles.

When Ikki was alive she entertained many people, regardless of their age. Even after death she contributed a lot of information to science. In April 18, 1988, Wayne State University in Detroit displayed a life-sized painting of Ikki for exhibition. The painting, along with the memories of Ikki, still continues to attract people to Detroit.

CHAPTER 8

OUR INTERVENTIONS

Elephants aplenty

One of the consequences of controlling poaching is population increase in animals. Many African countries are facing this problem of population increase in elephants. The countries that are affected with this problem include South Africa, Zimbabwe, Namibia, Kenya, and Botswana. One solution for this problem is to collect huge fees for issuing licenses for trophy hunting of wild animals, including elephants. In 2005, Namibia's sixteen protected regions for wild animals were set aside for twelve trophy hunting purposes, which brought an additional income of $495,000 to the country.

In the past thirty years, many countries that were supporting trophy hunting withdrew from this approach. However, Kenya is now seriously considering implementing this program again. For a trophy hunting of an elephant, they charge a fee of $10,000. This license is valid for three weeks. For a lion the fee is $3,500. For an African cape buffalo, it is $3,000. This country's elephant carrying capacity is only forty-seven thousand elephants. Now Kenya has an elephant population of 110,000 elephants to care for and support, with a growth rate of 5 percent. So, their plan is to set aside at least five hundred elephants for this purpose. They already have a store of twelve tons of ivory. They are also planning to sell these twelve tons of white gold (ivory) for the welfare of people and wildlife.

There were 4,500 elephants in one elephant sanctuary and now the population has increased to twenty thousand. Botswana has an elephant population of 120,000 elephants which regularly destroy agriculture crops (crop raiding) and residences of people. The government has the responsibility to protect these crops and control marauding elephants that enter human habitation. However, many scientists who know elephant psychology are saying that it is better to kill an entire herd rather than killing a few in several herds.

The Kruger National Park in South Africa is another place with an elephant population problem. The elephant population reduction plan was stopped in 1994 and the population increased from 8,500 to twelve thousand. If the population increase is not controlled, the ecology of the country will change completely. They are also predicting that nature will take over and control the population by way of diseases and famine. This type of nature's take over has occurred in elephants in Tsavo National Park in Kenya.

Africa has four hundred thousand elephants and produces four thousand tons of ivory, which doesn't even meet 1 percent of the demand of China. Hunting of elephants has been going on for many years. Still, a significant increase in the elephant population has occurred. So, elephant lovers are suggesting another method to control population. Although many are loudly screaming for control by contraceptives, there are no such practical methods with effective results available at this time. Some promising vaccines that can be given by darting are forthcoming.

Many elephants have been relocated to different sanctuaries, but the population increase is still continuing and is a big problem. Although illegal elephant hunting is controlled, most of the ivory on the market is coming illegally from those countries which claim to have successfully controlled hunting. This has been shown by DNA tests in recent years.

The communities that are victims of elephant attacks routinely say that they should be allowed to participate in the decision-making. Most decisions regarding controlling population are made by people who do not have any association with elephant problems. They sit in a safe place and make decisions. It is very unfair. Let the people who experience the problem make the decisions. The decision should be logical to the land and people. The beauty of nature is that its production capacity is reflected in all aspects of wildlife. So, relocating a few elephants to other places won't effectively solve the problem of population increase in these countries.

Elephant population control in West Bengal

Anything in excess can be bad. If there is an excessive elephant population, then it is highly unfortunate and is difficult to control. Among Asian elephants, 60 percent of them live in India. West Bengal, a state in India, is facing this situation. When the elephant population increases in the state's forests, the villages and nearby towns bordering the forests face threats from elephants. Estimates of elephant population indicate a slight increase in West Bengal. People depend on the forest for timber, gasoline, and livestock grazing. When the growing human population encroaches on the forest area, the habitat of elephants is fragmented and disintegrates.

Human and elephant conflict is at an all-time high now. Elephants seek more food and walk to the villages and farm lands to raid crops, causing problems for the people. The state government is requesting the central (federal) government's permission to capture these marauding elephants. West Bengal spends the highest amount for control of the elephant population among all the states in India.

Approximately six hundred elephants raid crops in the bordering regions of the forests. Almost a hundred people have been killed by elephants in one year. The property and crop destruction caused by this human-elephant conflict is estimated to have cost several millions of dollars. The southern region of the state is affected the most.

The law allows the killing of wild animals when they are a threat to people; however, if the animal belongs to a group of endangered species, then special permission is needed. Since elephants are included in the endangered species, special permission has to be obtained from the central government. Recently, the central government gave permission to kill nilgai or blue bull antelopes which caused a severe loss of agricultural crops in the area. Nilgai or blue bulls are one of the largest antelopes in India. The state had to shoot and kill almost two hundred antelopes there. The other side of the coin is that human population is also increasing in West Bengal and Bihar states of India. This increase in elephant population, along with destruction of forests in these states by human encroachment, produced a double-effect on elephants. Their population is increased and at the same time their habitat is decreased. On a global level, the rank of elephants on the endangered species list is ten. There is a general consensus that the overall increase in population has to be controlled not only in animals but also in people.

The federal government is proposing an experiment on immuno-contraception in elephants in West Bengal. This technique induces reproductive hormonal imbalances in female elephants using a vaccine. Although not tried in Asian elephants, it has been a success in African elephants. These vaccines are reversible and without serious adverse effects; one injection of vaccine lasts for approximately two years.

Underground passages for elephants

Readers must be wondering why underground passages are constructed for elephants. Elephants travel in herds from forests to countryside and also from one part of the forest to other parts of the forest. In this process they will be prone to accidents. In order to prevent stray walking and to direct the traditional migratory routes of wild elephants in the forest, it is customary to install electrified fences in many countries. However, these fences also cause life-threatening accidents to elephants. In addition to these dangers, poachers who regularly monitor these traditional migratory routes of elephants in the forests also attack and kill elephants for meat and ivory.

Surprisingly, the largest animal on the land is also killed by the largest vehicle of the land. When a train hits an elephant, the velocity and the mass of the train produce an enormous momentum, causing a heavy impact on the animal. In such cases, the survival of the animal is very unlikely. Usually the media reports such incidences with sad pictures of the elephant struggling for life. However, there are no permanent solutions in place as of today.

Trains accidents happen in many places in India. Some forest areas are designated as elephant corridors. In recent years, one accident happened in this area at night. The train ran into a herd of elephants which were crossing the tract. Five elephants —three calves and two adults—died immediately due to the impact. The adults were trying to protect the calves by surrounding them. Local people gave warning signals to the locomotive pilot using flashlights. The pilot was traveling at high speed and did not see the flashlight signals. The engine of the train was derailed. In this area, the railway line goes through 13 percent of the elephant corridor in Assam State. Animal activists say that human encroachment and animal habitat destruction force animals to deviate from the traditional route and come into the villages. Villagers, electrocution, and train-hits take a huge toll on elephant lives. In spite of all these tragic deaths, in reality, the elephant population increased in these areas last year.

It is interesting to note that Tamil Nadu state in India is coming up with a project for preventing such incidences.

The forest and wildlife department of the state is proposing to build an underground passage for elephants, especially in the border area of Kerala state and Tamil Nadu state, a well-known elephant corridor in south India. The exact spot for this passage will be at the border region called Madukkarai, on the outskirts of Valayar and Coimbatore towns. Recently, two elephants were hit by trains. The passage will be built in collaboration with Tamil Nadu forest department and Southern Railway of India. The officials of the railway and the forest department met at the Palakkad, a division center of railway, and came up with a plan to institute this project.

The curvy area between Madukkarai and Valyar is a thick forest and the department cleared this area recently. This was done to give the locomotive pilots a clear vision from a distance to see elephants crossing the train track. However, this did not decrease the accidents of elephants. Although they tried to reduce the speed of the train at this point, that did not do any good either. One week after clearing this area, another accident occurred, which suggests the problem still exists. They decided to dig an underground passage in this area so that elephants could go under the railway track. They are trying to reduce the expenses for this project using only minimal amounts of concrete and other expensive materials for construction. The railway track will be almost fifteen feet high above the passage. For thc time being, the government has started a patrolling service at this point.

Chinese-style elephant feast

The temples in Kerala State, India, particularly in the mid-Kerala temples, have a system where devotees can feed elephants as an offering to God.This is one of the most common offerings to God and the temple gets lots of donations for this purpose. However, when wild elephants destroy the agriculture before the harvest, people don't tolerate them. In olden days, it was one of the duties of the kings to protect the fields from wild animals such as elephants. This has been mentioned in *Artha Sastra,* one of the oldest books written by Koudillya (Chanakya), who was the chief minister of King Vikramaditya several centuries ago. Destruction of crops (crop raiding) by elephants is a common problem in countries with a large population of elephants. A few years ago, there was an international conference conducted in Colombo, Sri Lanka, on this issue. Around this time in the Eastern region of India, farmers poisoned and killed three to four elephants that came to raid the crop and to destroy the harvest. They even wrote the name "Bin Laden," the notorious terrorist leader, on the back of a dead elephant in white paint. The government suggested that farmers grow produce that is not usually eaten by elephants such as tobacco in areas that border the forest where elephants roam. Although effective, it is not an easy task for the farmers to implement.

Recently, a new method was tried experimentally in China to control crop raiding by elephants. This method does not involve cultivating crops that are disliked by elephants, but instead cultivating items that are liked by elephants. But farmers there are skeptical of this idea, so the government is taking a lead to implement this concept. The leader of this research project is a Chinese fellow, Mr. Aster. Two years ago, his coworkers came to India to obtain some practical expert training in handling wild elephants. They were also seeking help to capture elephants by the use of tranquillizers.

They plan to do this project as an experiment in Yunnan province. This is in the southern region of China, north of countries such as Myanmar (Burma), Vietnam, and Laos. The population of elephants in this area had reached significantly low levels to the point of extinction. This is why they got the attention to investigate the problems in elephants and conduct research to improve the situation. Special attention to these elephants was given and they started seeing good results. Twenty years ago, the elephant population in this area was eighty and now it has increased to three hundred. Along with this increase in population, elephant crop raiding also increased. Elephants came down to the fields from the forests searching for food. Usually, in Kerala State, India, moats or electric fences in the border areas are constructed between cultivating lands in the village and forests where elephants roam. The Chinese tried these methods with little success, so they came up with the new idea of cultivating crops that are liked by elephants in the border areas. The concept is based on the principle that elephants will be attracted to the more likable border crops than the crops cultivated by the farmers in the village.

Currently, the government has set aside seventy hectares of land for border crops that are preferred by elephants. For this type of "elephant buffet" concept, the government has to give four million Yuan (Chinese money) to twelve thousand families of farmers as a compensation for the use of their land on the border. The border crops are sugar cane and bananas. This "dinner hall land" is located on the banks of a river, where there is plenty of water. Therefore, after the sumptuous dinner, elephants can wallow in the river and enjoy life with the herd. Mr. Lisiyong, the director of this project, expects that the farmers' problems with elephants will be solved soon by this measure. It is anticipated that the proverbial saying "the elephant in the sugarcane field" is going to be an effective solution. We will have to wait to see the results.

Paternity rights in elephants

In this modern world, paternity in mankind is very important for many reasons. To name a few, it gives a person the rights for inheritance of ancestral property and for the right to claim one's progeny.

In Western zoos, the number of male elephants in total (either tuskers or males without tusks), are few; therefore, the mating records are easy to maintain. No dispute arises, at least in elephant breeding farms or zoos. This system is also good to avoid mating of closely related elephants to prevent inbreeding and related diseases. Artificial insemination has also started in the Western world in elephants. All these factors taken into consideration, paternity disputes in elephants are very unlikely to occur in the Western world. On the other hand, the situation is entirely different in some Asian countries. For instance, in Kerala State, India, both male and female elephants are routinely taken to the forests for timber logging. They belong to different owners and the elephants are sent to work based on their bid to get a contract. In their free time and during the night, the elephants roam around and graze in the forest. Recently, one female elephant found her partner, mated, and got pregnant. Then, a dispute arose among owners of male elephants regarding the paternity rights for the progeny.

A question may arise over what the importance is in these elephant matters. In the business world, rare and endangered animals and their products rank third in illegal international business today. The first rank goes to ammunition sales and the second rank goes to the narcotic drug deals. The elephant, being an endangered animal, is the primary reason why we need proof for paternity entitlements of a baby elephant. For example, the reputation of Thailand is not very good in terms of wild animals. A couple of years ago, Australia decided to import six baby elephants from Thailand for zoos in Sydney and Melbourne. According to the international treaty, a country can export only the animals that are born in that country and the export cannot be for business trade. However, in order to circumvent the trade law, Thailand argued that the elephant being an endangered species, Australia would be a better place for the protection of the elephant species. This deal was opposed by several organizations around the world. This matter reached Thailand's senate and also the Australian courts. Dr. Cheeran had to appear in Thailand's senate and the Australian court as an expert in elephant disputes.

The dispute was whether the baby elephants imported to Australia were born to elephants in captivity or born in the wild. Most of the elephant camps in Thailand are situated in the border lands of neighboring countries such as Myanmar (Burma) and Cambodia. Thus, a high intensity of illegal elephant trades take place by bringing elephants from Myanmar and Cambodia to Thailand, which then exports them, claiming the elephant is native to Thailand. In reality, some of them are born in Thailand and many of them are not. So, the dispute was about whether the baby elephants exported to Australia were really born in Thailand. The baby elephants were exported from the Ayutthaya Camp, which had more than 140 elephants. They showed the male elephants that sired the baby elephants to the author. But there were no records to prove this claim. This was the basis for the dispute.

While all these disputes were continuing, Thailand decided to export some baby elephants to China. This decision of Thailand prompted international enquiry and further disputes. Dr. Cheeran raised the question of why the DNA test had not been done for the so-called sires and the baby elephants that were to be exported. The senate gave a lame excuse that they actually wanted to do it and were just in the process of developing a standard DNA testing protocol. Since the techniques were in the early stage, they had not removed the "bugs" of the procedure and could not guarantee the results. If they did it in the present condition, it would lead to more problems and worsen the present dispute.

They introduced a new bill, which was approved. The minister in charge of the portfolio then was Ms. Nutopal Pattamma, who made a press conference about this new rule. According to this new rule, they are preparing a detailed list of all the elephants and their DNA fingerprints. When a new baby elephant is born, its DNA profile will be made and stored along with those of the other elephants. Elephant owners in different parts of the country should report the birth of a new elephant in their farms within seven days of the birth to the authorities. Previously, the owners were required to report to the authorities only when the baby elephant was eight years old. Similarly, if an elephant dies, that information should be given to the authorities. Before this rule, the owners need not report the death of an elephant at all. If death was not reported, owners could use the deceased as the sire of the newborn baby elephant. The minister also pursued opinions and modified suggestions from the public to improve the effectiveness of this rule.

Number plates for elephants

There is a practice of putting "chips" in elephants. A chip is used to identify an elephant accurately and to prevent fake transactions and exchanges. Identifying an elephant from a group of elephants is not an easy task. Many people usually wonder how you identify an elephant. Identification is a difficult process when all in the group look alike. There is a story about a learned man named Kakkasseri Bhattathiripad in Kerala State, India. He was very wise and it is said that he was endowed with the ability to identify each crow in a flock of crows. No one knows if this is true. The point is that even if he claims he identified each one, how could you verify and confirm his finding? The best way is to believe whatever he says. Identification of elephants is much more complex. Just because of the difficulty, there are many incidences where con artists were successful in fooling many innocent people. There were instances when an elephant without life insurance was dead and the owner tried to claim insurance money, showing the records of another elephant. Installing a chip is a procedure that is meant to end such foul practices by scam people. A few years ago, there was a government project to "chip" all elephants in Kerala. Now it is reported that the project is completed and all elephants in Kerala State have this electronic chip installed.

Assam State, India, had also completed this electronic chip project the previous year.

What is this microchip? The chip is installed under the skin of the elephant and provides the identity of the elephant using chip-reading equipment. The microchip system has two components, a chip and a chip-reader. Using a reader, one can read the chip through the skin of the elephant. Thus, the elephant can be identified. A microchip, as the name indicates, is a small electronic device. The device has a diameter of a grain of rice and a length of one centimeter, and is placed inside a Plexiglas capsule. This capsule is inserted under the skin of the elephant. Conventionally, it is placed under the skin on the outside of the left earlobe. The reader component of the system can read the information from the chip if placed within ten centimeters. The reader is the size of a cell phone.

Usually, information in the chip is in a code containing numbers and letters, moreor less like the number plate of a car. Codes can look something like this: KN 123456789 or 123456789 T or 4 B 123456789.

This chip system is used not only in elephants but also in other animals. Now it is being used in house pets such as dogs.

Microchips will prove the ownership of the elephant. An analogy is the registration book of a car. Thus, it can be used to catch smugglers who bring elephants illegally from forests, other states, or even from other countries. Even in Kerala State, there are several identification cases in courts to prove the ownership of elephants.

Thus, microchips help to properly identify elephants without any error. In India, the government takes the lead to implant microchips in elephants in all states. Some people do not show interest in microchipping their elephants. However, it is a big help for owners and breeders who follow the law of the land. When you buy a car or any other vehicle, we usually note down the engine number and chassis number in addition to keeping the registration book. This type of proper bookkeeping increases the value of the car and makes transactions go smoothly. The same principle applies with microchips in elephants.

The important matters in installing microchips include:

1. Microchips should be placed in the same location in all elephant. The conventional location is outside (external) of the top left earlobe.
2. The reader equipment should be available to the official in charge of identification.
3. There should be a data base (data bank) to store all this information.

Many readers of this book probably know that such a system exists in the central government to prevent theft of cars in India. Let us hope that such a system will be in place for elephants at the state and central government levels. Many other countries are far ahead of India in this matter.

Family planning for elephants

The population of people and elephants are increasing in geometrical progression. The increase in elephant population has been responsible for the destruction of crops and loss of life in many places in India. The same problem exists in several other countries too. A few years ago, radio collars were introduced to assess the home range of elephants. Seven years ago, Dr. Cheeran was instrumental in putting 'radio collars on elephants in the northeast regions of India, close to Bhutan, where human-elephant conflict had been a serious problem in recent years.

As mentioned before, there are mainly two types of elephants, African and Indian elephants. Among the African elephants there are two subtypes, large and small. The total number of African elephants is estimated to be between four hundred thousand and six hundred and fifty thousand. Very few African elephants are in captivity. This number may be somewhere around seven hundred to one thousand. Most of the captive ones are in the zoos, primarily in North America and Europe.

The population of Asian elephants is smaller compared to African elephants. The Asian elephant population is limited to thirteen countries, spanning from the region of southern China and covering the entire area of southwest Asia. The elephant population is only forty thousand to fifty thousand. Almost one-third of this (fifteen thousand) are captive elephants. Therefore, all Asian countries have a great responsibility to take care of captive elephants.

The program for controlling elephant population is directed towards African elephants. The population increase in many African National Parks started destroying forests. There is a shortage of grass, leaves, bark, and bushes, which are the usual foods for wild elephants. The uncontrolled increase in population is continuing to destroy the ecosystem of small plants as well.Therefore, the African government started to kill elephants in large groups. In the wild they live in large herds and most of them in the herd are blood related. To avoid their mental stress, a strategy to kill the members of a family (herds) was adopted. In the beginning they started killing by shooting, but later started using tranquillizers. This program faced a lot of criticism from the elephant lovers and their organizations all over the world. Now the government has started a program to transfer them to other forests instead of killing them.

An elephant will eat about 250 kilograms of fodder (food) a day. This will give one an idea of how much of the forest can be reduced by a herd of elephants. Between 1966 and1994, forest officers killed sixteen thousand elephants in Krueger National Park alone in South Africa.

Recently, scientists came up with a new idea. Instead of killing or transferring them to other forests, measures for family planning can be applied to wild elephants. In zoos, this has already been applied in other wild animals. However, application of this system in elephants has made a lot of practical problems. One way of applying this system in people is by installing hormone pills under the skin. The dose for such hormone pills is based on body weight. Considering the huge bodyweight of elephants, such a pill will have to be the size of a soccer ball. This was really an inconvenient method and indeed a practical impossibility. Another method in animals is by using contraceptive vaccines. In zoos, this vaccine is used for sterilization and requires only one milliliter in volume. It is also easy to inject it. However, in wild elephants, this is not an easy task. Although the volume is only one milliliter, it has to be given subcutaneously. It cannot be given into the muscle. Subcutaneous injection cannot be given by a dart gun. Now the scientists have come up with a technical solution to this problem. The solution they suggested in elephants is vasectomy, a technique that has been very popular in humans, though not that popular in animals. Dr. Mark Stetter, the chief veterinarian for Walt Disney World Animal Kingdom, came up with the idea and initiated the implementation. In a video he showed one-and-a-half-meter long equipment and claimed that it is very effective for the implementation. The surgery that utilizes a laparoscopic video monitor will take two hours. In order to do the surgery, the wild elephant has to be tranquilized first. There are more than a thousand wild animals that need the surgery.Taking these two factors into consideration, people are skeptical about the practicality of this idea.

Vietnam War strategy for catching poachers

Scientists are trying to use the strategy that was used by Americans against guerilla fighters in Vietnam to monitor weapon transactions of the forest poachers and smugglers. This strategy will help the authorities to determine how poachers and smugglers are getting weapons for attacking animals and forest officers. The national park areas spread many thousands of kilometers. So, it is not easy for the forest officers to find thieves and poachers in every nook and corner of the park. For instance, the national park in Kenya is an area of more than four thousand square kilometers. Just imagine trying to monitor the activity in such a wide area by few forest officers—it is practically impossible.

Let us look at the "Vietnam Technique" used by America. During the Vietnam warfare, America wanted to find out who was supplying weapons to the guerilla fighters. At that time, weapon trafficking went through the Ho Chi Minh Trail. So America installed several instruments called "trail guards" along the route of the weapon trafficking to guerilla fighters. This instrument is only twenty-five centimeters long and detects any iron-containing item when it goes within its range, and sends a signal to the American soldiers. Hunters of wild animals will carry large shot guns, machetes, axes and knives, so trail guards were installed in areas where animals come for drinking water in river banks and also where food is available in plenty, because these are the places poachers will be looking for. Since the forest officers know all these places, they can come prepared in no time. So with this equipment, catching smugglers red-handed was almost sure and easy. At the same time, casualties of the officers can be reduced to the minimum by the use of this method. So, this technique came as a blessing in disguise for the forest rangers.

However, during Vietnam war-time, these trail guards were not very effective. At that time, to send messages, they used planes that flew over these trail guards. Today the system is improved. The instrument can send messages via satellites. These signals sent by the instrument will come immediately back to earth and reach the exact location using the Global Positioning System (GPS). So, with this improved system, all animals, not only elephants but other wild animals, can also be protected. In addition, use of this system also prevents unexpected attacks on forest officers by poachers.

The World Conservation Society has come forward to protect chimpanzees in the southern region of the Congo. Through the use of these modern trail guards, confrontation of forest officers with smugglers can be reduced and casualties among the forest officers can be considerably minimized. Since the information about the illegal hunters is received accurately, the officers can encounter them fully prepared with arms and the help needed for confrontation. In 1994, the National Park in Kenya found more than two hundred dead bodies of elephants killed by illegal hunters. From this, a reader can assess the gravity of the situation caused by smugglers, ivory poachers, and illegal hunters.

It is interesting to note that this technique is spreading rapidly to other countries. In China, a common illegal activity in several mountain valleys is to catch cats (Chinese mountain cats) using iron cages. Use of these trail guards prevents this illegal activity as well. It is nice to know that a technique used to find illegal weapon trafficking is finding its way to help nature and wildlife. This news is actually comforting to every nature-loving person.

Rats to save elephants

The Zimbabwe Ministry of Defense is taking an active interest in saving elephants from land mines. The Ministry entrusted a charity organization named Apopo to train rats for identifying and locating landmines. Just like the bomb squads use dogs to identify bombs, they use rats. These rats belong to a breed called African giant pouch rats. Now their nickname is "hero." They can locate and identify landmines and other explosives by sniffing. They are preferred to dogs because of their light weight. The chances of them activating the landmines are very low, practically none.

The great Limpopo Transfrontier Park is spread over three countries, including South Africa, Mozambique, and Zimbabwe. These "hero" rats are used now to locate landmines along the elephant trails of the park. Elephants routinely walk through the park, resulting in the formation of a trail. Landmines are usually found on these trails. Apopo has a bomb squad of three hundred members. They provide all the protection for the rats. So far, they have cleared more than one hundred thousand landmines and explosive bombs. This park area poses a threat not only to elephants but also to people who use this area for international business. If Zimbabwe is able to clear this area completely of landmines and other explosives, this area could be developed as a beautiful tourist center. Although rats were used for identifying landmines, their activity allowed access of healthcare workers to this area. This helped the Department of Ministry to identify and provide treatments to more than twelve thousand people afflicted with tuberculosis.

Elephant meat, an expensive food

It is believed that elephant meat has been used for human consumption since prehistoric times in Africa. The history records show that in 1456, Al vise Cadamosto, a Venetian explorer, traveled to the Gambia River basin where the locals served him roasted and boiled elephant meat. He even took a salted elephant ear when he returned to his country and presented it to the prince as a souvenir. In 1790, Francois Le Vaillant visited a tribe in the interior of Africa where he was served elephant foot for breakfast and he found it very tasty. In 1869, Paul de Chaillu reported that he was served with a big pot of elephant meat in a country near the equator in Africa. The meat was tender because it was boiled for more than a day. He also had the opportunity to eat smoked elephant meat, which was tough, dry, and tasteless. The famous explorer Dr. David Livingstone reported in 1864 that in Mozambique he enjoyed a breakfast of elephant foot porridge. It is said that in 1868, Sir Samuel Baker, a Victorian naturalist, instructed his associate on how to barbecue an elephant foot by digging a pit in the ground, burning wood in the pit, placing the foot in, covering pit with mud paste, and leaving it for thirty-six hours. He said that one foot would feed fifty people.

Killing elephants for meat was a common practice. In recent years, when elephants were killed for population control in Krueger National Park in South Africa, elephant meat was sold for human consumption. Once the local people in the park had what they need, the excess meat was sold outside. Then it became known to all around the world. The leftover meat was processed and canned for sale at a later stage. Presently, elephant meat is consumed by people in many countries, including those aboriginal tribes in the north eastern region of India.

The craving for elephant meat caused some problems in some countries in the African continent. Since the elephant is an endangered species, meat is not commonly available; however, it is available in the Central African Republic in food markets along with meat of varieties of monkeys, chimpanzees, and deer.

Thus, in our modern times, the poachers have two reasons to kill an elephant. In addition to the high price of ivory, elephant meat is also a good commodity. In a conference in the Netherlands where an extensive debate took place to determine whether to ban ivory sales or not, a good amount of information was revealed about the illegal marketing of elephant meat. They say more value was obtained for meat than ivory. After killing an elephant, the poachers take the ivory and smoke the meat by burning green bushes. Since the smoked meat stays good for a long time, they can take the meat conveniently to the market at a later stage.

The price of ivory in Africa is around $20 per kilogram and the price of elephant meat is about $10 per kilogram; however, the quantity of the commodity is different. From an elephant, one can get about two to three tons of meat. Even a small elephant will fetch 2,500 kilograms of meat. So, from ivory one can get more than $1,000 per elephant, whereas from meat one can get $25,000 to $30,000 per elephant, easily. Therefore, poachers kill elephants even with small tusks, because meat becomes their attraction. In addition, it is sad to say that a rare variety of small elephants seen in some areas of the African jungle have become targets for these poachers.

License for elephant hunting

It is customary in African national parks to issue a license for hunting large animals such as elephants and wild buffaloes (seen in South Africa) for a fee. The license is given by the government. When hunters kill animals for trophy, the animals are usually large and old. The government and wild animal rangers estimated that there won't be much loss of wild animal population by issuing hunting licenses. The fee thus collected for a license ranges from $750 to $1,000 for an above average sized elephant. The proponents of the scheme have planned to spend the amount collected for maintenance of wild animals and also for the welfare of local people. However, because of the pressure from the animal lovers all over the world, this plan was temporarily halted for some time. Now some African countries have come forward to open this system again. They suggested that a fixed number of hunting licenses should be allowed per year for the benefit of wildlife maintenance.

Zimbabwe is the country that is applying pressure at the international level. An article that came out in a Zambian daily mail newspaper on January 27, 2007 reported that the American government should take an initiative to encourage license issuing policies of those countries to hunt elephants for trophy. The American government had banned its citizens from trying to get licenses for hunting elephants. This trophy hunting is not allowable according to the CITES international treaty. Those who support trophy hunting claim that it is not only to stop the unwanted increase of elephant population but also to help the betterment of wildlife maintenance.

The government is trying to introduce the license issuing policy in the region of the Zimbabwe-Zambia border. Recently, the minister in charge of this portfolio introduced this matter at the International Hunters Annual Conference in Reno, Nevada. However, when Zimbabwe was willing to allow five hundred elephants to be hunted, Zambia did not agree with it. They don't want to allow more than twenty elephants.

The government of Zimbabwe claims that there are several benefits with this kind of hunting license issuing policy: the increase in elephant population can be stopped; it reduces the damages to agriculture caused by elephants; danger to people from elephants can also be considerably reduced because when population increases, they begin to come down to the villages in search of food resulting in crop raiding; and the monetary gain from issuing licenses can be utilized to improve the welfare of wildlife.

In the years 2001 to 2005, the government had to kill 115 elephants just to stop destruction of farmers' agriculture and to avoid compensation payments for crop raiding by elephants. If they would have allowed this number of licenses to hunt, it would have raised more than a million dollars for the benefit of wildlife.

The American government has agreed to consider the recommendation of Zambia regarding issuing hunting licenses.

Merciful elephant hunting

The readers must be raising their eyebrows at how there can be mercy in hunting to kill for trophy. Hunting to kill is also called game hunting. The following is a narration of one classic merciful elephant hunting.

This event took place in a national park in the African continent. The elephant hunting team was ready with its preparation, one day before the event. The team gathered information on elephants, such as the size of the elephant, its head size, and length of the tusk. The very next day, in early morning before the sunrise, the team members were ready to go. Elephants would be seen only in the early morning hours or in the late afternoon hours close to sunset. In the noon hours, because of the hot weather, elephants would be resting under isolated trees surrounded by the tall grass of the thick forest.

The hunting team started with long hunting rifles and an experienced guide to show them the paths in the thick forest. The team came to help a wealthy man from America who showed interest in hunting and shelled out a lot of money for this game hunting. He was also walking along with the group. As usual, the fog slowly started clearing up in the early morning hours. Because the forest was full of tall grass, one could see an elephant coming from a distance if they were standing on raised ground. During the fog in the evening, one could also see elephant herds moving like a mountain of rocks from a distance. White tusks of the elephants glisten when sun rays happen to fall on them. Elephants have a tremendous capacity to recognize smell from far away distance. Therefore, the team had to move closer to the elephant only after knowing the direction of the wind. The guide felt the direction of the airflow by throwing a pinch of sand from uplifted hand. The team started moving forward after getting the direction of the wind. So, the team took all the measures to avoid elephants getting their smell. The team's main purpose was to help the wealthy man to shoot and kill the elephant. If he succeeded, the team members would be rewarded generously for their help.

Since elephants have poor eyesight, the team was able to go very close to the herd. When the team reached close enough to shoot, the guide gave the signal to the shooter. The most significant moments of the hunting expedition start at this point. The panic starts when the darter pulls the trigger and the dart really hits the animal. That is an unexpected and surprise moment for the elephant. At this moment, the elephant took a couple of unsteady, wobbling steps and finally fell down. When the animal fell down, the photographer took the photo of the shooter with the fallen elephant, and a picture of the entire team with the fallen elephant. They took the maximum number of photos. Then they measured the length and the circumference of the tusks.

At that time, a second team with a veterinary doctor examined the elephant and announced to the rest of the group that the animal was not dead. This is because the first shot was a tranquilizer. Then the doctor gave the antidote for the tranquilizer. Everyone moved away from the elephant.

The first sign of recovery is the flapping of the earlobes and movement of the trunk. To rise up to the standing position is usually a very difficult process for the animal at that time. It can stand up only after several attempts. Finally, when it stood up, it looked around and tried to grasp the situation, as if thinking, "What happened?" Then it moved its earlobes back and forth, which are indications of normal recovery, and walked away from the scene after shaking its head and tusks.

Later, both teams met in their camp and discussed their experiences. The shooter's satisfaction was reflected on his face. At that time they presented to the shooter a pair of life-size tusks made based on the measurements they got from the elephant. These fiber tusks look very real. Most of the time, these fiber-tusks are "readymade" in advance for everyone's convenience. This was followed by several photo shots.

Thus, the hunting was a great success with a happy ending. The passion of the shooter was fulfilled. He was able to shoot down an elephant. At the same time, the elephant did not die, and could be used for another trophy hunt. The park owner got a hefty amount. The shooter got a pair of tusks to keep as a center piece in his living room in America. Both team members got excellent tips. The veterinarian pocketed a handsome amount. Thus, everyone involved in this adventure was very happy. Now this type of hunting has become a big business.

This type of hunting is seen in many places in Africa. They call this "Green Hunting." They developed this craziness into a big business by exploiting the basic instinct of man which we call it a "thrill." The reward for this thrill is the pair of tusks in his living room.

When the tranquilizer dose is inadequate

A few years ago, Dr. Cheeran had to collaborate with a government-sponsored project to transfer several elephants from the Doddabetta Forest in Karnataka State, India, to Nagarhole Wildlife Sanctuary in the same state. Tranquilizing wild elephants is a difficult endeavor. When the government built a dam in Hemavathi River, a few elephant herds were trapped on both sides of the river. The trapped forest areas were called Kutteppura and Doddabetta. These areas were well-known for coffee plantations. It was an usual occurrence that the wild elephants would come down to the coffee plantations and maraud through the plantations, destroying the plants. When the project was initiated, the chief wildlife warden in charge of forest and wild animals was Mr. Appayya. He decided to transfer the elephants to Nagarhole Wildlife Sanctuary near Mananthavadi of Kerala State. Probably this project was one of the first of its kind in India at that time. The Minister's cabinet officials contacted Dr. Cheeran, who was the only expert in drug immobilization of elephants in India at that time. With much thought, the author gave the green signal. He always knew that it was not going to be an easy job and one with a lot of accountability and responsibility.

There was a special course at Mysore Zoo given to forest rangers and veterinary doctors about the principles and methods of elephant tranquilization. Overall, this course had a tremendous impact in the execution of the project involving the transfer of elephants. The intent of the project was to transfer all elephants safely from the trapped location to the Nagarhole Wildlife Sanctuary, a distant place in the same state. The darting (tranquilization) had to be performed by going close to the wild elephant, which was in the standing position on the ground. An experienced tribal individual was hired for darting. The individual had to be bold enough to go close to the wild elephant and had to be a sharp shooter. The government officials were able to find and hire an experienced tribal individual who was familiar with the forest.

Although Dr. Cheeran has several hilarious and adventurous experiences in tranquilization of elephants, this particular one was unique and needs a brief narration. The government officials had a rough idea of the number, gender, and size of the elephants in that area. One of the elephants was a huge male with long tusks. Dr. Cheeran gave the tribal guy a dart gun filled the normal dose of the tranquilizer. Since he knew the area very well, he walked faster than the rest of the team. By doing a "cat walk" he reached very close to the elephant and darted him. The author was on the top of another captive elephant and he could hear the sound of the shot. Immediately, he could hear and see the elephant screaming and shaking the trees in the vicinity. It was a very scary feeling. Anything could happen. The author and the associates started shouting to give the signal to the shooter. Usually, when this is done, the darter on the other side has to shout back, too, which is called the "return call" to help locate the darter. This is the usual practice of communication in the forest when you cannot see each other. But to everyone's surprise, there was no response from the darter. The team was anxious and got worried. How come the tribal fellow wasn't responding? All the scary thoughts came to their minds. Something must have happened to him. Is he still alive? Did the animal kill him? Almost thirty minutes lapsed. Amazingly, the darter suddenly appeared from the nearby bush. At that time, they realized out why he did not shout. He was very close to the elephant. Not only that the animal was not down yet. The elephant was wobbling and still in the standing position. It did not move, though. Dr. Cheeran had another dart gun with only one more dose. He was afraid of using it because the elephant had already gotten a normal dose, which should have knocked him down. Another dose probably would kill him. There was no other alternative. Because the tranquilizer was in a dart syringe, he could not take some drug out. So, Dr. Cheeran gave the sharp shooter a gun with the normal dose to use on the animal. The team (Dr. Cheeran and associates) climbed down from the captive elephant and walked along with the darter with the antidote ready. The author noted that if the animal ran towards them, the sharpshooter could easily climb to a tall tree, but the team could not. However, he felt in his mind that because the animal had already received a normal dose, his pacing would be limited. The elephant was not down because of his large body weight and size. With this thinking Dr. Cheeran and the associates were able to walk along with the sharpshooter.

When they reached closer, they found that the wild elephant was still in a standing position but wobbly. The sharpshooter did not wait for a second. He fired the second shot. As it hit the elephant, it became alert one more time and tried to run, but because of the effect of the first dose he fell down after two steps forward. Dr. Cheeran rushed to the animal because the second dose could kill him. He was under intense pressure. He gave the antidote injection immediately. The dose of the antidote he used could block 25 percent of the effect of the total tranquilizer dose (both doses combined) immediately.

At the time, Dr. Cheeran took a deep breath to relax. He had been worried the whole time. If the animal died there would be extensive government enquiry, because this elephant was the best in the entire forest. He wanted to check the respiration and he tried to lift the trunk. That was when he really felt the weight of the trunk. Since the animal was tranquilized completely, the trunk was a dead weight. He placed a small piece of cotton at the tip of the trunk and counted the airflow movements as well as the chest and abdominal movements.

After some time, he was sure the elephant wouldn't die of the tranquilizer double-dose. Only then was he relieved of the tension and stress of the project operation that day. Later, this elephant was relocated safely.

Elephants: Smuggling and being smuggled

The third most important business in the underworld is the smuggling of endangered animal species and their products. The first rank goes naturally to the large-scale ammunition and the second rank to the illegal drugs. In the third-ranking business, endangered animal smuggling includes elephants. Many of the elephant camps in Thailand are located on the border of Myanmar and Cambodia. This is said to facilitate smuggling of elephants and the whole world is watching the wildlife export of Thailand, particularly to Australia, with suspicion.

A few years ago, Dr. Cheeran had a chance to visit an elephant camp in Ayutthaya (another name for Ayodhya), the old capital of Thailand. This camp has 142 elephants. Dr. Cheeran arrived there when they were expecting the birth of a baby elephant. A female elephant had completed the gestation term and was due any day. The owner of the camp came to see the elephant. He wanted to test whether it was going to give birth soon. In order to do that, he first lifted the tail of the elephant and made a fist and gently hit the perineal region (the area below the tail) of the elephant with his forearm. Then he announced to the onlookers that the elephant was not going to give birth that day. Later, it turned out to be true. During his stay there, Dr. Cheeran had the privilege of seeing elephants mate and deliver. However, could not say for sure whether all the baby elephants living there were born natives. Some of them could have been smuggled into the camp.

In the previous chapter, there was a mention of exportation of baby elephants by Thailand to Australia. This received so much publicity because of international attention. There are several cases of this type of illegal activity taking place regularly in Thailand. However, they are carried out secretly and silently, and do not go to higher levels of scrutiny, media coverage, and publicity. Cases are "hushed up" before it reaches that level.

Let us see how they use elephants for smuggling drugs. This happened a few years ago in Cambodia, where they use captive elephants for illegal drug trafficking. The smugglers secretly keep large quantities of illegal drugs (heroin, cocaine, and other expensive drugs) wrapped in heavy duty plastic bags inside the animal (rectum or vagina) after tranquilizing them with the help of veterinarians. The mahouts do not walk along with them or sit on their backs. They give silent hand signals to the agents of the smugglers. It looks like a couple of elephants just walking through the forest and does not generate any suspicion to the authorities. When the elephants reach the destination, the smuggler team removes the drugs with the help of veterinarians. The elephants will get sweet treats, such as unrefined sugar, tender coconuts, and other freebees. This makes the elephants very happy. These activities continued routinely for a long time, until the authorities got suspicious of this activity. Eventually, many smugglers are trapped and caught by the police.

Thus, elephants are smuggled and used for smuggling as well.

CHAPTER 9

WILD AND CAPTIVE ELEPHANTS

I am a wild elephant (My side of the story)

I CAME TO THIS world after staying in my mom's womb for more than twenty-one months. When I was born, I was one meter tall and weighed one hundred kilograms. When my mom was giving birth, my aunts and my grandmas were staying close by. It was a family affair and was like a big festival. Everyone was happy to receive me.

Within a few minutes of my birth, I located the nipples and tried to get Mom's breast milk. In the beginning, I was able to drink only for half a minute because my muscles for sucking were weak. When my muscles got stronger, I was able to drink milk for a longer time.

Although I was able to stand up within a few minutes of my birth, my walk was kind of wobbly; however, within two days I was able to put each step forward with steady force. Since I was not able to walk along at the speed of my herd, they slowed their speed and stayed close to me. They did not go far away from me because they were afraid of leaving me alone, which would increase my vulnerability to wild predators. The herd did the same thing when one among them got sick or was unable to walk, always trying to help the sick and weak. Sometimes, they even tried to raise the fallen members, continuing to do this till the weak got better and healthy. They would resume their normal walking speed only when everyone in the herd was able to walk together.

My mom would have been very sad if I had been stillborn. Still birth babies are buried in the same way as adults who have died. If anyone dies in the herd, they don't leave the place until a ceremonial burial is performed. All the relatives gather to bury the dead one. The burying process involves completely covering the dead body with dirt, leaves, and small branches of trees. If I am going to have a brother or sister, it will take more than four or four and a half years.

When I was able to walk and keep up with the rest of the herd, we went to drink water from a lake. When I saw water I was so excited and I ran into the lake and jumped into the water. When I started playing in the water, all the elders told me not to do that but to drink the water first when it is crystal-clear. When you play, the water gets stirred up and it becomes muddy and drinking muddy water is not healthy. Whenever there is an opportunity, elders give advice to young ones.

When we were on a trip, we had to cross a river. The water flow was pretty strong. That time, two large elephants asked me to stay between them. The largest one stood on the side that water flow hits first (upstream) then the other large elephant stood next to me in the down- stream. They did this till I reached the other side of the river. This is how they protected and helped me to cross the river. They knew that I was only a baby and would be vulnerable to accidents due to the river currents.

When summer came, the river was completely dry and no water could be seen in the river. The elders in our group moved to different areas of the river and placed their feet, pressing down very hard. They seemed to be listening to something. That is the time someone in our group told me that we have the ability to sense the flow of water current underneath the ground. That means we can "hear" through our feet.

Once we find the water flow underneath the ground, we make a small ditch by stomping on the ground. We remove the sand and dirt with our trunks. Usually elders in our group do this. When water starts coming to the surface, we wait a few minutes for the flow to settle. When the water settles and becomes clear, only then do we drink it. The other animals also benefit by us finding the source of water. They also can drink this water when we leave.

We can also communicate with other elephants by pressing on the ground. These sound waves cannot be heard by people. The frequency range is five to twenty-four hertz. These sound waves can travel underneath the ground and between the trees for a pretty long distance. These types of waves are also produced during thunder and earthquakes. Therefore, we can "hear" earthquakes through our feet much earlier than hearing by our ears. We can also "hear" the tsunami waves coming long before people can hear or see them. This helps us to move to a safe place long before flash floods and tsunami disasters arrive.

I was told that the scientist who discovered our ability to sense soundwaves through our feet was O'Connell of Namibia. Similarly it was Katherine Payne who investigated our ability to monitor rare soundwaves. This lady scientist even wrote and published a book entitled *The Silent Thunder*.

Since we have strong, pillar-like legs, we are able to sleep while standing. Normally, we sleep only in familiar surroundings or in places that we can trust with regard to our safety. This is why only a small number of people have seen us sleeping on the ground. When we are terribly tired we can even sleep leaning onto a tree. I heard the elders say that there was one among us in captivity with joint disease and he slept leaning on a tree for eighteen months!

If we stay long enough in one place and eat all the vegetation, that whole area will be devoid of plants; therefore, we keep moving from one place to the other. We can eat and walk at the same time. We cover a vast area by walking. People call this path we produce *anatheri*, which means elephant path. It may be a surprise for many of you that the oldest grandma in the group is usually the leader of the herd. This is true for all of our herds. She knows all about the food, crops, and water, which are essential for our survival.

Our brothers usually leave the herd when they are fourteen to fifteen years of age. The reason for this is to prevent mating among the members of the same herd. Those who moved out from our herd, as well as from other herds, make a new herd of bachelors. We, the babies, normally continue to breastfeed for about three to four years. There is no rule that we have to drink only our mom's milk. We are allowed to drink milk from any mom in the herd who is wet nursing. Recently, an older captive female of our group brought an orphan baby from the jungle to the Marumala camp of the forest department to feed milk. In that camp there were many females lactating.

When there is a shortage of food, we split into many groups and when there is plenty of food after a rain we gather again. We express our happiness by a special loud sound and also stomping on the ground. We also greet each other by entangling our trunks or putting our trunks into each other's mouth. This is very similar to the handshake in people or feeding cake during happy occasions. In addition, we sniff and smell the area just above the forelimb nails. There will be something like a sweat drop. This contains special chemicals called pheromones, which give a specific scent.

Our smelling ability is more powerful than our ability to see. For example, we can smell jackfruit from a long distance. Our poor vision is the reason why a hunter can come close to us by knowing the direction of the wind. Wind can bring the smell of the hunter to us and we can sense the presence of the enemy easily. To avoid our detection, hunters carefully determine the direction of the wind and approach us from the opposite side. By doing this they can come very close.

The females in our society do not show any outward excitement during the "heat" period or estrus, as cows do. However, they excrete some strong-smelling pheromones in the urine. The smell of it can be sensed by bull elephants through a gland that is located in the upper portion of the throat in the mouth. This gland is soft tissue similar to the tender fleshy portion seen inside the palm nuts. By smelling the urine of a female, the male can identify which one is in heat and will be receptive to them. When he recognizes the female, he will call her for mating. Both will move away from the herd to a secluded place for mating. Their courtship and eventual mating will go on for three to four days. During this time they mate several times. Each mating will take only a few seconds or less than a minute, but they mate several times in a day. The mating process is similar in all quadrupeds and during the mating period, a special muscle helps the penis enter the vagina of the female. Since the vagina is located very low in females, this muscle is important for successful mating. This muscle is absent in other animals. If giving birth is a family affair, mating is a secret matter between lovers. Just like some other animals, we also have special preferences for our sex partners and like humans we do not have any special season for mating, it can happen year round.

The fight among the males for a common lover is not rare. Sometimes the fight will last for two or three days. It is not always true that the tusker will win during a fight between a tusker and a makhna (male without tusks). The loser will run away from the fighting area with his tail raised when he gets defeated. When the loser starts running, the winner will give another prick with his tusk on the butt of the loser. Sometimes, the loser's tail will be bitten off. So, if you happened to be in forest and if you see a male with a cut off tail, invariably he must be a lover who lost the fight with his rival.

Our dental condition is unique. We have only four molar teeth at a time. Two upper and two lower on each side, with a total of four molars. They erupt at four months, six months, three years, six years, twenty years, and forty years. It is not actually an eruption as seen in people. It is a replacement in a unique way. Instead of the worn out tooth falling out or shedding as a new one erupts in the same place, as in people, the worn out tooth is replaced by the tooth that comes from behind. The new tooth pushes the one in the front and then the old tooth falls out.

Elephant carrying palm leaf

Our food consists of more than one hundred varieties of vegetation. The usual foods are grass, leaves, climbing vines, small branches of plants, and bark of some trees. We can eat all vegetation in all tiers of the forest. These have to be chewed well because they are very fibrous. Since the last set of teeth gets worn out by age sixty, sixty-year-olds cannot eat any vegetation in the forest. They eventually face death by starvation in the wild; however, in captivity they get cooked food like rice and can live longer. Recently, a captive grandma elephant is reported to have her eighty-seventh birthday in Kerala State, India. She is considered the oldest living elephant today.

The ridges on the surface of the tooth increase as the replacement progresses. For example, the first formed tooth will have four to five ridges, whereas the tooth on the twentieth year will have twenty to twenty-nine ridges. The ridges on the teeth of the lower jaw will have more ridges than those on the upper jaw.

Captive elephants in Africa

Elephants were captured and tamed in Asia during the Vedic period, long before Christ. There are records showing that they were used in battle. In the Hindu epic story of Mahabharata, a story of battle between two related clans, there is a description of a well-known elephant by the name of Ashwathama. This battle is believed to have occurred in 1500 to 500 BC or even more. However, in Africa, capturing of elephants and taming them started several years later. There are some references to tamed African elephants used in battle. Hannibal, 247-182 BC, used elephants to resist invasion of the Roman Empire. History tells us that he started from a territory called "Gaul" in Africa, then went to Italy, crossing over Alps Mountain. This happened around 219 BC.

Hannibal was a Carthaginian. Carthaginians were business professionals. They did not have their origin in Africa. So, historians believe that Hannibal brought elephants and their mahouts from Asia by ship to Iraq first and then to Gaul in Africa by land. So, these historians assume that Hannibal's people were not interested in capturing and taming elephants in Africa.

In 1988, historians wanted to re-enact the trip used by Hannibal, taking the same route he used. They used three Asian elephants named Tally, Dido, and Batamen. Both Tally and Dido completed the trip but Batamen became lame and abandoned the trip and was brought home later.

In order to commemorate the victory, the Carthaginian General Hannibal introduced silver coins, which portrayed elephants and those who rode them. When experts analyzed the proportions of the height of the people and the elephants, they determined that the elephants had a height of less than eight feet. These types of small elephants belong to the species *Loxodonta africana cyclotis*, which are seen in Africa, suggesting that Hannibal actually used African elephants, not Asian.

The strategy in using elephants in battle was to induce fear in the opponent's army. But many times, when elephants were wounded, they caused more problems for their own army. It is said that those who rode the elephants even carried weapons to kill those elephants running amok to avoid further damage to their own army.

There is proof the Roman Empire used elephants in military tactics and also in parades. This indicates that large numbers of elephants were used in the Mediterranean region for various purposes. It is believed that the eastern regions of the Euphrates and Tigris Rivers were inhabited by plenty of wild Asian elephants.

There are no reports that Carthaginians and their neighboring countrymen, Egyptians, used elephants for any other purpose. After the fall of the Roman Empire, the use of elephants in battle faded and subsequently vanished.

The Belgian King Leopold II was very much interested in using elephants in battle. Before he became the emperor, he visited Ceylon (Sri Lanka) in 1865 AD. That is the time he learned about the use of elephants for various purposes. People used cattle, donkeys, and horses for travel in most of the countries in those days. Elephants were more resilient.

Although wild elephants were available in middle African countries, they had never been used for travel or any other purpose because they were not captured and tamed in those days. King Leopold got an idea that elephants would be useful to capture the Congo. He decided to do a risky experiment using elephants in battle and was willing to pay for the expenses.

Thus, King Leopold bought four elephants, two females named Dosankalpi and Pulmulla and two males named Sundergred and Naderbux from India. He shipped them from Bombay (now Mumbai) to Africa. On June 1, 1879 they arrived at the Chinsura Seaport in Tanganyika (Tanzania). They were disembarked a few yards from land. The elephants waded through the waters and when they arrived on land, the people who came to see them were wonderstruck. The local people could not believe what they saw. However, the excitement did not last long. The trip to the interior of Africa was a disaster. The elephants started dying one by one. Leopold did not give up on his idea and tried again, ending with the same results. However, he kept his dream alive in his mind about the use of elephant in his African colonies.

Later, in the beginning of twentieth century, Asian elephants were exported to Africa. Sir Heskth Bell, then Governor of Uganda, was the one who initiated it. He wanted to use elephants for hunting but that idea also failed because the elephants did not thrive.

Later it was the missionaries who tried to tame African elephants. In 1890, Gaben Lefernance initiated this in the place called Vas. His first trial was to tame a male African elephant which was trapped in mud. In Africa, both male and female elephants have tusks. The elephant that underwent the taming experiment was given the name Frits. Lefernance and associates were successful, and made use of Frits to help them around the area where missionaries lived.

When Leopold heard the news that missionaries tamed an African elephant, he was excited and thought his dream came true. He became interested in taming African elephants and decided to tame elephants in his African colonies.

Later, around 1890, King Leopold sent Commander Julep Lipum to the Congo. Lipum's goal was to capture African elephants and tame them. Ten years later, he started a training center for elephants in Africa. He started a plan for capturing African elephants by using the technique used in South India. This was supervised by Mr. Kirvongue, the tribal head in Azadae. The South Indian technique is to make a big pit and hide it with the use of split bamboo and leaves and sprinkle soft lose dirt or sand. When elephants walk on it they fall down to the pit and can't get out. Unfortunately, the plan failed because the elephants that fell into the ditch were either rescued by other elephants or died during the fall. Lipum tried other plans as well. He and his associates tried shooting into the air to create chaos in the herd. When the elephants start running out of fear, baby elephants would be separated from the adults and easily caught by roping. If some adults did not run away, he shot and killed them.

By the end of 1902, they got four baby elephants for training. These baby elephants were allowed to be with the experienced elephants. These experienced elephants' job was to help in taming the baby elephants and also to calm them down. The trainers were called Karnacks. With the use of experienced elephants they successfully trained baby elephants. The training progressed as the baby elephant grew. The training was based on love and affection.

In the beginning, the basic commands given to the baby elephants were simple, such as walk, stand, turn, and hold trunks. However, as the training progressed, baby elephants were used for carrying weights and pulling carts. When new forests were cleared, elephants were used to plow the land.

The Congo in Africa was still a colony of Belgium. According to Captain Keith Caldwell, the Congo had more than fifty elephants in 1925. Of these fifty, nineteen were working adults and twenty-five were young adults who could do light work. The remaining six were baby elephants that were undergoing training. As of 1918, Albert I was king of Belgium and he gave his full support to the elephant facilities, including financial help. In order to improve the training he even brought mahouts from India and Ceylon (Sri Lanka). Captain Caldwell did not have a good opinion about the way these mahouts trained elephants. Two out of five baby elephants died because they could not handle the bad treatments of these mahouts. Their punishments were severe and included beatings, cutting skin with spears, and even starving. Later, because of their disagreements about work-related habits, these mahouts were sent back to their homes. However, these mahouts were responsible for the organizational systematic training. They established the framework of the daily routine for the trainee. They proved that man should establish the dominance over the animal in order to tame them. Those foreign mahouts used commands in their language, which were foreign to the local workers. This was changed to the local language in subsequent years.

Between the years of 1927 and 1929, this elephant camp was moved to the northeast corner of Belgian Congo. This was a favorite place of hunters. Later in 1938, this camp became the world famous Garamba National Park. Here, it flourished well and the elephant number reached a total of eighty-four. This park remained the same until the Congo became independent. By that time, the number of elephants was decreased to fifteen. Domestic political unrest and the notorious "Simba" mutiny were responsible for this reduction. The rebels captured and held the Garamba National Park under their control. So, Karnacks (mahouts) escaped to the jungles with their elephants and took refuge there. Finally, the elephant number came down to four. Capturing of new elephants stopped. At that time, the average age of the remaining elephants was thirty-five. Although many international organizations came forward to help this elephant camp, none could succeed. In order to expand the Garamba National Park, three more baby elephants were captured and added to the existing elephant group. Although foreign tourists decreased, the authorities understood that using elephants for a joy ride is a profitable business. Now this business is considered a primary source of income and is slowly flourishing.

The authorities brought three tamed African elephants from different zoos and circuses to the southwest region of Botswana. They also brought three adult elephants and seven baby elephants. These were leftover elephants when several herds of elephants were moved from South Africa's Krueger National Park. Thus, they made a group of elephants that were tamed. This was a big step forward to start an elephant riding club for tourists. They charged $3,625 for one week's ride. For any extra person, they charged an additional $1,100. Now those who rent elephants are increasing. Although their rate is fairly high, the interest in an African forest ride is increasing. Unlike the Asian forests, which are thickly filled with tall trees, African forests are flat planes without large trees. So elephant rides in the African forest gives a clear view of large areas and sightseeing is more fun. In this case, an elephant ride beats a motor vehicle ride. The view is also much better on an elephant. Since the elephant ride is a slow-moving process, it allows better sightseeing. Various other animals can be seen. The wealthy business men expect a huge role for captive African elephants in tourism in Africa. The only drawback in this business is the huge capital investments and lack of expertise in elephant training. In addition, maintaining an elephant for at least fifty years is a big commitment. These factors are holding back some of the foreign business entrepreneurs.

Some experts are coming up with new ideas and asking why African captive elephants can't be used for timber logging, construction projects, and patrolling national parks, like they do with Asian elephants. It is expected that eventually they will come up with more uses for captive African elephants.

Current affairs of captive elephants of Kerala State, India

Almost all elephants in Kerala State, India, are either captured from the Western Ghats forests or brought to this state from other states of India. Very rarely they are born in captivity. Western Ghats is a mountain range that lies along the western coast of India. It extends from the Mumbai area all the way down to the southern tip of India. India's western border is the Arabian Sea and the southern border is the Indian Ocean. Kerala State lies between the Arabian Sea and the mountain range, Western Ghats. Western Ghats mountain range is a thick rainforest area which has wild elephants, tigers, leopards, monkeys, etc.

Capturing of elephants in the wild from the Western Ghats was banned by the government in 1972. The Government of India also banned tree clearing (felling) and logging in forests. This produced a crisis about the use of elephant in the forests, particularly in the northeast and east regions of India. In the northeastern region, elephants are mainly used for wood logging. The changes caused by this ban meant many elephants were "unemployed" and the owners had to sell many of them. However in Kerala, the demand of elephants was not affected as much as in the northeastern regions of India, because elephants are used widely in temples. So there was a surge of elephants from those affected northeastern regions to Kerala State. Many elephant owners sprung up in Kerala because there was a high demand for elephants in temples and other religious functions. The state of Kerala had only two hundred captive elephants, but incoming elephants that came from other states of India caused a rise in captive elephant in Kerala to eight hundred. The influx of elephants from other states has come to a steady rate now. The present elephant population of the state is only four hundred to 545.

Captive elephants are used in Kerala for different services. They are used mainly in Hindu temple functions. They are also used in timber logging, which comes next to the temple demand. They are also used in Christian Churches and Mosques for various activities. Elephants have an important role in the Hindu religion and culture. They are revered in the religion. The Hindu deity Ganesh, one of the popular gods, has a human form with an elephant head. He represents wisdom and removes all hindrances and obstacles. Another deity, Devendra, the god of gods in the heaven, has a white elephant by the name of Airavatham as his vehicle. The temple activities include processions around the temple areas and from one temple to another temple.

There is one temple in Kerala which once used 101 elephants at a time for certain functions. This is a yearly function called Pooram. During the procession, the tallest elephant will carry the idol of the lord and the other elephants will carry symbols of the lord. Usually the total number of elephants will be an odd number, with the tallest one is in the middle and an equal number of elephants on either side. All elephants will be decorated with gold-plated front covering from the top to almost two-thirds down of the trunk. In addition, four people will be on the backs of each elephant: one person to hold the idol or symbol of the lord; a second to hold a pattukuda, a colorful umbrella usually made of bright red silk cloth and lace work or small bells; the third person to hold Alavattam, a shield made of finely shaped and cut peacock feathers arranged in a circular form with a handle; and the fourth person to hold venchamaram or Flails, a white flowing tufts to fan the idol of the lord. Based on the music and beating of drums, the people on the top, except the one holding the idol, will stand up and sit down on the back. They have to keep their balance when they stand up because there is nothing else for them to hold on. At that time, the elephant will stand still and won't move. The activities in the temple will have a competitive spirit among people belonging to different areas.

It is a matter of prestige to get the tallest elephant for the function, therefore the demand and price for the tallest elephant is great. Thus, the story of Guruvayur Keshavan, the famous tall and gentle elephant (previously mentioned) is an example to illustrate this competition. The leaders of the group are willing to pay an exuberant price to hire tall and gentle elephants like Keshavan; therefore, the demand of tall male elephants never went down in Kerala. Even after the ban on capturing elephant from the Western Ghats, the people of Kerala got elephants from other states, particularly from the northeast regions.

Pooram Festival

Elephant influx from other states in a short period of time caused many problems in Kerala State. First, the demand for experienced mahouts (trainer and caretaker of elephants) rose. The chief mahout has to be an experienced one. He has the complete control and dominance over the elephant. He should have worked for years as an apprentice to a senior fellow over a period of six to ten years. Since there was an acute shortage, many inexperienced assistants who did not complete the apprentice course became chief mahouts to many elephants. They did not have the traditional knowledge of animal training based on the elephant's psychology. The second problem was many of these elephants were trained in different languages. It is true that in India each state has its own language. When elephants trained in a different language came to Kerala, even the experienced mahouts found it difficult to deal with those "foreign" elephants. Malayalam is the language of Kerala. It took years to retrain the elephants to the language of Kerala. Many mahouts, especially the fully experienced ones, did not have patience to wait that long. This produced frustration in elephants and mahouts, which resulted in abuse of the elephants. Since the demand for the use of elephants increased, the owners did not want (or couldn't afford) to miss the golden opportunity available to them. So, owners pressured the mahouts, who in turn pressured the elephant, who could not learn the language that easily. Everyone, the owner, mahouts, and the elephant, became frustrated by this situation. The elephants started reacting to this aggressively and the mahouts without elephant-managing skills in such condition reacted aggressively, often with drastic punishments. Unfortunately, this became a vicious cycle.

The third problem was the circumstance of the hype of "Pooram mania." Every individual wanted the temple festival of his own local area to be the best in the state. They formed organizations to collect money and increased the amount of fireworks associated with the temple activity. Overall, temple activities and festivals in Kerala state increased tremendously. Many temples that did not have such activities in previous years would suddenly come up with elaborate activities involving elephants. Not only that, they even increased the number of elephants in the same festival. So the use of elephants increased throughout Kerala. Each elephant, especially the famous ones, had to be in festivals continuously, one after the other without much rest. The brokers, or the agency that rent elephants from the owners, pay a set amount for the season. In order to make maximum profit, they bring the elephants to festivals as many times as possible. Not only are the elephants hurt by these people, mahouts are also hurt because they have to go wherever the elephants go. To alleviate the stress and tension, mahouts take refuge in liquors, especially in cheap illicit liquors. Some mahouts give liquors to their companion elephants also. They (elephants and mahouts) do not get enough rest or sleep during the Pooram season (summer time), worsening the scenario to a disaster.

In addition, male elephants should not be taken to festivals when in musth. Usually, they will be kept secured; however, it will cause a huge loss in income. During the "Pooram mania" season, some mahouts take elephants showing signs of aggression to the festival anyway. Mahouts won't report the animal's condition to the owner or to the customers. These elephants with initial signs of musth are very vulnerable to provocations in the festival, such as misbehavior of other elephants or people or fireworks. Their border-level musth becomes a full-fledged one during the festival.

All these contribute to uncontrollable elephants running amok in temple functions and causing damage to property and to the lives of people and other animals. It results in instances such as mahouts being gored to death, and some cases the public as well. Many times experienced mahouts have to be brought from distant places to manage these animals because the local mahouts do not have the experience and skills to manage elephants in such conditions. To add to this problem, there are not any experienced veterinarians to tranquilize these aggressive elephants with the use of capture guns, syringe projector, or dart guns. Very few veterinarians are trained in elephant health.

Exercise is an important factor in the well-being of an elephant. In the wild they walk several kilometers in search of food and water. This exercise keeps them in good condition.

In captivity they are tied to strong trees all day and night with access to food and water. The only exception is the festival season. They should be walked five kilometers (one hour walk) to get proper exercise. This routine practice builds up a good relationship between the mahout and the elephant. However, for most mahouts, walking the elephant is extra work and, therefore, they ignore or discourage this. Ignoring this routine practice by mahouts, particularly the inexperienced ones, prevents formation of an emotional bond with their elephants, which could result in disobedience and misbehavior on the part of the elephant. This further leads to cruelty to elephants by mahouts. An inexperienced mahout believes that inducing fear is the only way to dominate the elephant.

In Kerala, the festival season lasts for about six months, of which the peak is only three months. This provides seasonal income for the owner of the elephant but the rest of the time, almost six months of the year, there is no income from the elephant. During this period mahouts take leave to visit families. The elephants are cared for by part-time workers. This off season is a time of neglect for the animals. Elephants do not get proper scrub baths, an important part of their well-being. At this point of time (2018) there are four hundred to 545 elephants and more than 2,500 festivals in Kerala State, which suggests how difficult is for elephants and mahouts.

Elephant Scrub Bath using a hose

Elephant Scrub Bath in a pond

Currently, the Forest Department of Kerala Government has taken strict measures and implemented rules to make a better life for elephants and mahouts. Temple functions with elephants are prohibited during the hot time of the day, between 11 a.m. and 3 p.m. The public has to keep a distance from the elephants during the procession and ceremony. There is a limit to the number of elephants a temple can use in a festival. This considerably decreases the use of elephants. All these restrictions are implemented for the welfare of the elephants. However, eventually it is going to hurt elephants, because many owners cannot afford to keep them because their income is drastically reduced by these rules.

Wisdom Speaks

From their experience and knowledge, the authors give some observations on elephant for the benefit of readers and elephant lovers.

Elephants are highly intelligent and family-oriented animals. Elephants are like us. The role of the grandma is very important in raising the babies. They have many human-like characteristics. They are very compassionate animals. They observe everything happening around them and store that information in their memories. Their ability to identify a person or animal by their odor is excellent. Their response to love is amazing. Even during musth, they recognize the people who give them unconditional love and they respond to them the same way. They have many abilities and talents. They have good endurance in swimming, they can hear and communicate through their feet, and detect water underground, and they can smell to detect enemies (or friends) from a distance. Their talents include artistic drawing capability, remembering complex commands, recognizing their own reflections, and using tools. The ability to use tools is one the qualities that is linked to intelligence. Elephants can use chains or small wood logs to protect themselves from other intruders or to keep others at a distance.

1. Elephants in captivity will swing their chains when they do not want anyone to approach them. This applies to the mahout who approaches to tether them.
2. The elephant will bring all his chains in front of his forelegs to prevent the mahout from chaining him.
3. During mild sedation (hypnotic trance) elephants will recognize the voice of their primary mahouts but they will refuse to obey his commands at that time.
4. The sound of chains will alert an elephant. So, if you want to take the chains close to him, carry them in a bag.
5. If you are a veterinarian or someone who is going to manipulate him, make sure the elephant is lying

down and hobbled. Otherwise he will recognize you by your odor and will stay in a standing position.

6. The elephant recognizes people and other animals by smell, not by sight. An elephant sniffs by turning the trunk to the desired direction to detect someone's approach. Elephants have poor eyesight.
7. Since their eyes are on the side of the head, elephants have a blind spot in the front. Usually, the tusks are pointing upward and divergent. When they try to gore a person, there is a chance of not getting injured. On the other hand, when an elephant with downward directed tusks attacks, he will impale the victim. In elephant parlance, a person with unpredictable temperament is nicknamed a "downward directed tusker".
8. If you try to move the tethered elephant to shorten his reach, he will recognize it and go anticlockwise to get the previous length of the chain.
9. Tuskers will use their tusks as levers to break chains. Elephants used in timber logging are smarter in this art.
10. Elephants are given treats for their good behavior, such as completing the bath or returning from a festival or parade. They keep this memory every time when they complete a task and come to the same place for the reward. Usually treats are given by the ladies of house near the kitchen area. They come to the kitchen area.
11. Elephants can quickly identify the darting person. As soon as the dart hits, they will turn and look at that person and try walk towards you to charge you. Sometimes, they may even start walking backwards looking at the person who darted him.

12. Elephants can imitate sounds. Those that live near the railway stations imitate the sound of the train. Those who live near the farm imitate the sound of the farm animals.
13. Their expression of grief is similar to humans. Rage and stress are expressed by elephants. They remember and mourn loved ones. When one elephant in the herd is injured or shot, the others do not run away. The rest of the herd stays there to help the disabled elephant.
14. The oldest female in the herd is the leader, not the tusker. She teaches the young ones the manners and lifestyles of the herd.

ABOUT THE AUTHORS

CHANGARAM VENUGOPAL is a veterinarian and hails from Kerala State, India, where elephants are widely used in festivals. While a student, he was exposed to various ailments of elephants in veterinary clinics and through his master's degree research project examined various pharmacological agents for immobilization of animals. After MS and PhD degrees from the US, he continued a postdoctoral fellowship at Harvard University. In 1981 he joined Louisiana State University as a faculty until he retired in 2014 and is currently holding the Professor Emeritus status. He was awarded the Beecham Award for Research Excellence, Distinguished Faculty Scholar Award, Distinguished Alumni Award, Best Teacher Award by the class of 2011, and a Fulbright Teaching Scholarship, as well as a patent for developing a peptide for airway diseases. He has authored more than one hundred scientific publications and is a fellow of the American Academy of Veterinary Pharmacology and Therapeutics.

DR. JACOB V. CHEERAN, a veterinarian cum pharmacologist, served as the head of the Pharmacology Department of Kerala Agricultural University and the Head of the Department of Wildlife Sciences in the College of Forestry. He was also a professor and Chairman of the Elephant Studies Center and a member of the Steering Committee of the Project Elephant and of the Central Zoo Authority of the Government of India. During his career he has tranquilized more than 500 elephants and has presented topics on elephants at several conferences around the globe. Later he was awarded a patent for an instrument that administers medicines to wild animals from a distance. He retired in 2000. During his career he has been invited to several countries, including USA (Smithsonian), UK (Royal Veterinary College), Germany, Switzerland, Netherlands, Thailand, and Australia to give seminars on elephant management, elephant immobilization, and musth in elephants, and also to attend court hearings as an elephant expert. He is a member of several international organizations including the Asian Elephant Specialist Group of IUCN and is a fellow of National Academy of Veterinary Science. He has written several books in his native tongue as well as in English and many of his personal experiences are depicted in this book.

THE US Review of Books

The Incredible Essence of Elephants

by Changaram S. Venugopal and Jacob V. Cheeran FriesenPress

book review by Jennifer Hummer

"Environmentalists and ecologists consider the elephant a corner stone of the environment because they are associated with plants and animals equally."

Written by two veterinarians, this book explores every aspect of an elephant's life. The authors' ardent love for these magnificent and compassionate creatures comes across immediately in this captivating work. As well as being veterinarians and experts on elephants, both authors have a long list of achievements awarded to them from institutions across the globe, and each holds impressive titles. For example, Venugopal is a distinguished professor and author. Meanwhile, Cheeran is a pharmacologist as well as the head of the Department of Wildlife Sciences in the College of Forestry. Although Venugopal and Cheeran are both highly educated and accomplished, their writing style is straightforward and simple enough for readers of every level. The authors have included photos and diagrams to back up their research and findings. The photos, including the book cover, are heart-warming and will most certainly melt an animal lover's heart.

The book discusses every element of the elephant's life, from their physical make-up and biology to their intuition, loyalty, and love for one another. The authors have included both Asian and African elephants in their research, comparing and contrasting their similarities and differences in easy-to-read formats. The authors also discuss the ancient history of the elephant, whose majesty and mythical allure date back centuries. Although known to many Americans as merely circus animals or zoo exhibits, readers will come to learn that elephants have been revered and celebrated for thousands of years.

Filled with rich and unique findings, the book also offers insight into an elephant's inner life. Their problem-solving abilities are similar to humans, and they appear to have funerals for their dearly departed. Elephants even recognize their own reflections. They are the largest of all land animals, and their brains are strikingly similar to the human brain. They also experience post-traumatic stress disorder. Sadly, humans are the elephant's only natural enemy in the animal kingdom. A particularly heart-wrenching chapter discusses heroin smugglers who get elephants addicted to the drug to control them and use them to smuggle more of the product. It is both infuriating and hopeful to learn about human interactions with these amazing creatures. Although protected by many cultures, there are still plenty of vicious smugglers who exploit and murder them for their tusks. Perhaps it is only by reading books such as this one that people will understand the importance of protecting these incredible creatures.

Although there are plenty of facts and figures about the elephant included in the book, the material is creative and fun to read. One of the chapters is told in the voice of a wild elephant, which is sure to delight readers of all ages. Readers will also learn about some of the most famous elephants in history, including Raja (king), an Asian male elephant so beloved by the people that the president of Sri Lanka declared him a "treasure of the nation." Another enchanting section of the book discusses the importance of grandmothers to baby elephants. Human grandmothers will be undoubtedly delighted to learn that the survival rates of baby elephants are much higher when they are looked after by their grandmothers as well as their mothers. Researchers, parents, young children, and students alike will find so much to love in this complete guide to elephants.

RECOMMENDED by the US Review

www.ingramcontent.com/pod-product-compliance
Ingram Content Group UK Ltd.
Pitfield, Milton Keynes, MK11 3LW, UK
UKHW062257290726
14090UKWH00017B/739

9 798892 160087